THE POTTER'S TALE

COLONSAY

-==========-

Balnahard
Bay

• Balnahard

Kiloran
Bay

Uragaig •

Loch an
Sgoltaire

• Colonsay
House
• Kiloran

Eilean Olmsa

Primary
School •

Pigs' Paradise
Kilchattan •

Graveyard •

Loch Fada

• Riasg Buidhe

• Glassard

Glen
Cottage

Port Mor •

The Pier and Harbour

Hotel •
Scalasaig

The Lighthouse

Machrins Bay

Golf Course •

Airport

• Machrins

• Milbuie

• Baleromindubh

Loch
Cholla

The Temple
of the Glen •

MacPhee's
Cross

• Balerominmor

Ardskenish •

Garvard •

The
Strand

• The Hangman's Rock

St Columba's
Landing Place

Poll Gorm

ORONSAY

Oronsay
Priory

• Seal Cottage

Seal Island

Eilean
Ghaoidmeal

THE
Potter's Tale
A COLONSAY LIFE

DION
ALEXANDER

BIRLINN

First published in 2017 by Birlinn Ltd
West Newington House
10 Newington Road
Edinburgh
EH9 1QS

www.birlinn.co.uk

ISBN: 978-1-78027-473-7

British Library Cataloguing in Publication Data
A catalogue record for this book is available from the British Library

Typeset in Bembo at Birlinn

Printed and bound by Grafica Veneta
www.graficaveneta.com

CONTENTS

ILLUSTRATIONS

ACKNOWLEDGEMENTS

I am very grateful to all those who have encouraged and helped me in any way to bring this book to eventual fruition, not least Ian and Sandra MacAllister, Keith Rutherford, Irene Christie and Hugh Andrew and his hardworking team at Birlinn. I really don't deserve the wonderfully written and flattering foreword penned by one of my heroes, Jim Hunter – but I'll take it, with huge respect and gratitude. I am particularly indebted to Carol and 'Peedie' McNeill for their unwavering hospitality, kindness, support and general indulgence, aided and abetted on sea and land by David and Jan Binnie. Finally, my beloved other half, Helen, deserves a special mention for bearing with me throughout the book's long gestation period.

Di Alexander, 'The Colonsay potter' as was, October 2016.

DEDICATION

For all my loved ones
and
for anyone with a special place in their heart for the magical
Hebridean islands of Colonsay and Oronsay

FOREWORD
by
James Hunter

This book repays a debt – the debt its author feels he owes to the Hebridean island of Colonsay where Di Alexander, his wife Jane and their baby son settled in 1972. Their being there was not untypical of the times. A number of young southerners, often of hippyish outlook and artistic bent, were then coming to the Highlands and Islands in search of the good life – consisting usually of a mix of self-employment and self-sufficiency. Round every corner, we natives sometimes said, you'd find a pottery, a potter and (frequently) a goat. Put like that, our take on these newcomers might seem cynically condescending. In part, no doubt, it was. But in my case anyway, other emotions were involved. I was of Di's age-group. But I was one of innumerable Highlanders who'd headed elsewhere in search of a higher education and such job opportunities as it might open up. Eventually, in the 1980s, I'd make it back to the Highlands and Islands. But ten or fifteen years earlier that seemed unlikely. Then I was very much a product of age-old Highland thinking (less prevalent now but by no means extinct) to the effect that anyone wanting to get on in the world had better begin by getting out. This, or so we were encouraged to believe, might be regrettable but it was also unavoidable. Hence the envy, or perhaps it was resentment, some of us felt on seeing other young folk, of whom Di and Jane were two, demonstrably giving the lie to the notion that the Highlands and Islands had nothing to offer – by moving north, not south, and by setting up home in the very places so many of us were quitting.

At a couple of generations remove, Di is himself a product of our centuries-long Highland exodus – his surname deriving from Caithness fish-curers and boat-builders who were among the beneficiaries of the Victorian herring boom that turned Wick into one of Europe's busiest fishing ports. Just before 1900, one of those Alexanders, Di's paternal grandfather John, won a scholarship to Edinburgh University where he graduated in medicine – prior to marrying and going off to work in West Africa. A Scottish connection would be re-established when Di's father, Donald, took up a university post in Dundee. But reinforcing this connection, Di stresses, was Dr John Alexander's decision, on retiring from the south of England practice he'd acquired on returning from Africa, to set up home with his wife Hilda at Weem near Aberfeldy. There Di holidayed occasionally with his grandparents, and there he began, he says, to feel the urge (acted on as described in his opening chapters) to make a life for himself in the Highlands and Islands.

I didn't know Di then. That would change when I went to Skye to work for the Scottish Crofters Union, now the Scottish Crofting Federation. This was in the mid-1980s when Margaret Thatcher's ministers, or so it was feared, might be tempted to axe the taxpayer-financed Crofter Housing Grant and Loan Scheme which advanced to crofters a part of the cash it took to get new homes built on crofts. How, we wondered, might we best make a case for the scheme's retention? What we needed, I knew, was expert advice on housing policy, and it was in this connection I first heard mention of Di Alexander. Initially, I envisaged someone female. Then, when I'd been put right on Di's gender, I thought he must be Welsh. In fact Di, who grew up in Berkshire and Wiltshire, owes his first name to parental fascination with classical Greece. Which is not, by the way, to suggest that Donald and Budge Alexander were more engaged with the distant past than with what was going on around them – Donald's still widely shown film footage of the impact of the 1930s depression on South Wales miners being a pointer to his having had much the same commitment to social justice as is evident in his son's endeavours on behalf of a whole host of Highlands and Islands communities.

When Di became one of the people who helped the SCU secure the continuation of the Crofter Housing Scheme (which, we demonstrated to initially sceptical Tory politicians, was a highly cost-effective means of enabling families to become home-owners), he was working for Shelter. Afterwards he became a key figure in, first, the Lochaber Housing Association and, then, the Highlands Small Communities Housing Trust. Between them, these organisations have provided – and are still providing – hundreds of new and affordable homes in localities where such homes would otherwise have been lacking. This achievement, Di stresses, is by no means his alone. That's true. He's had lots of hard-working collaborators. But Di's contribution has been huge all the same – not least because of his having developed all sorts of insights into the crucial connections between housing provision and wider well-being. A place where there are houses to buy at reasonable prices, or where young folk in particular can afford to rent, is a place that can flourish and grow. A place lacking these things, as all too many Highlands and Islands communities know to their cost, is doomed to economic contraction, population loss, stagnation and decline.

Di's understanding of those issues, together with his long-standing determination to do something about them, he attributes (as is evident on following pages) to his years in Colonsay. This, then, is his thank-you to islanders who both received him and his family very warmly and who, though this would take time to become apparent, did much to shape Di's life, his outlook, his philosophy. And not just his.

Between 2010 and 2015 the First Secretary of the Treasury in Britain's then government, a Conservative-Liberal Democrat coalition, expended a great deal of energy and political capital on winning a fuel-duty discount for those Hebridean and Highland communities where the effects of distance and disadvantage are constantly aggravated by fuel costs far higher than those prevailing in urban localities. First Secretaries of the Treasury do not generally bother themselves greatly with such matters. That this one did stemmed from his upbringing. At one point in this book he features as a little boy adding to the stresses and strains surrounding his younger sister's premature arrival in a Colonsay cottage by getting himself into the cottage's chimney and coating himself from head to toe with soot.

There is nothing of the adult Danny Alexander in what follows. Neither is there much about his father's life after Colonsay. This is not that kind of book. What Di has written is an often lighthearted, but nevertheless deeply felt, memoir of what a young man made of a small Hebridean island – and, just as importantly, what that island made of him.

Although this would become evident only in retrospect, the same young man was in at the start of much the most transformative thing that's happened to the Highlands and Islands in my lifetime – this being the way that, from the 1970s onwards and for the first time in centuries, many more people have moved into the Highlands and Islands than have left. We're much the better for those people being here. We're much the better too as a result of what Di Alexander has been about since he left Colonsay. For all of that, as well as for this fine piece of writing, *Moran taing, a Photter* ('Many thanks, Potter').

1

I Know Where I'm Going

The very first time I laid eyes on Colonsay I barely even knew its name, far less that it would, soon enough, become my home and my mentor.

It was a sunshine-with-showers afternoon in the early summer of 1971 and a long-haired, self-absorbed, 25-year-old ex-art student, male and clearly a late developer, stepped off one of Bertie Bowman's hard-worked buses at the Clansman Restaurant and Pub in Pennyghael, a tiny settlement at the gateway to the Ross of Mull which is the long, south-westernmost arm of the Inner Hebridean island of Mull. The deposited figure wore maroon velvet flares frayed at the knees and a collarless working man's vest, which he had dyed, rather fetchingly he felt, a brick-dust pink. His general appearance was underscored by a somewhat dilapidated pair of moccasins which had never been watertight and were now proving even less so. A fairly typical product of the time and place of his upbringing, the new arrival was hoping to be met by Alasdair MacDonald, the man who had placed a small ad in the Personal Columns of the *Times* – which then still took up most of its front page – seeking a potter who would also double up and help him fish lobsters from his creel boat.

I just about qualified for half of this intriguing job description as someone partially trained as a studio potter (Wimbledon School of Art, late 60s, Certificate of Industrial Ceramics, only just). The ad appealed strongly to my romantic and escapist tendencies, which included the fond belief that I had always been miscast as a denizen of the over-domesticated south and south-west of England, where I had been raised and schooled and where I was then engaged in a subconscious exploration of my career options as I worked on a crushing machine for a firm of Wiltshire building contractors.

On health and safety grounds alone I knew that I needed to get off the crusher and start moving, quite possibly to the wild Highland roots on which I had some claim and which had always attracted me. Besides, the all-female-staffed Inniemore Summer School of Painting in Carsaig, where I was now headed with my new boss, seemed to offer much better prospects for an active social life than the narcoleptic West Country backwater in which I had become becalmed.

As my new and agreeably eccentric boss drove me in his well-worn kilt and shiny red Morris pick-up van along one of the narrowest and most inviting of single track roads (the ones which have tufts of grass growing up the middle), my senses were buzzing with the anticipation of what Carsaig would have to offer, and from the deep pleasure too which the then unfamiliar but spectacularly beautiful island landscape had been serving up ever since I had climbed on and off the Mull car ferry from Oban.

But the steep and dramatic descent from the road's seven-hundred-odd feet high point into the hamlet (a farm, two mansion houses and a few cottages) of Carsaig took my breath away just as surely as it had and has done to countless visitors before and since. For, falling away precipitously from the narrow single track, spreads a monumental, terraced, semi-circular amphitheatre formed from ancient volcanic rock that cradles a luxuriantly green and graceful valley, and there, beyond the ocean's lapping edge on the slate grey sands of Carsaig Bay, stretches the shimmering, deep blue sea of the southern Inner Hebrides (as viewed on a good sunny day, of course, but such it more or less was) with its scattering of magical isles: furthest away to the south the substantial islands of Islay and Jura; nearest at hand, and though still ten miles away seemingly close enough to touch, the islets known as the Isles of the Sea – or the Garvellachs – and to one of which that most famous Hebridean saint of all, Columba, habitually retreated to clear his mind of anything but God. And there in the middle but off to the right a bit of this vast and spellbinding seascape and looking small and isolated in its ocean surround, lay the little island of Colonsay which, with its, from that angle, concealed and interconnected little sister, Oronsay, were just ten miles long and not more than three miles wide between them as I would, eventually, come to discover.

And although I had no idea then that I would be going to live there, it didn't take very long before I knew who I would wish to go with me. For, within a few weeks of taking up my new duties at Inniemore Lodge I had fallen well, truly and headlong for the loveliest of all the nice girls who were employed to do the chores there; making sure that the guests' beds were made, sheets washed, meals prepared, rooms cleaned, everything set up so that they could spend their days learning to paint under the kindly eye and expert tutelage of Alasdair's wife, the wonderful painter Julia Wroughton.

Jane was 19, tall, titian-haired and as close as you would ever be likely to come to seeing Botticelli's Venus in the flesh, albeit now reincarnated in jeans and T-shirt and speaking modern English rather than Renaissance Italian. She shone from the inside too and but to see her was to love her. I, in response, radiated hot waves of more than purely spiritual interest which, heaven knows why, though it is true to say there were hardly any other potentially suitable male options readily available, were unexpectedly requited.

We did what lovers do on their journeys of discovery, including getting to know Carsaig and its environs as well as each other. After-work visits to the pub in Pennyghael were part of the pattern and there we got to know the resident locals rather than the transient artists and visitors who stayed with us for a week or two in Inniemore's secluded paradise. Whenever we ventured back over the crest of the hill from our Carsaig enclave we encountered the more typical island world, bubbling away unobtrusively but ever ready to share its day-to-day life in the friendliest of fashions and, if you happened to be in the right place at the right time, its – to us outsiders – unfamiliar enchantments. These were features of a more discrete but distinctive community which had its own strange tongue, infectious music and a wealth of local anecdotes and traditions; and though the language, called Gaelic but pronounced 'gallick', was totally incomprehensible – though fascinating – to me and my companions, the music and the stories were tailor-made for direct enjoyment by anyone, not least our young and curious selves. I lapped it all up and was hungry for more.

Never more so than on a Saturday night when the handful of older, Gaelic-speaking locals who lived within striking distance of the bar would congregate for a plurality of convivial drams matched by an equally generous sharing of stories and music with whoever else happened to be there, no matter where they hailed from, and that included the motley gaggle of that summer's new intake of seasonal workers to the locality. There was Pennyghael-born and bred Duncan Lamont, a renowned piper and soldier who had fought in both World Wars, and his brother Hugh who was equally famous locally as a bard – a composer of songs – in their mother tongue, even though it was then only spoken by Mull's older natives. There was Niellachan who always came with his fiddle, and old Tom, our nearest neighbour from Carsaig Farm, who would drive over the hill with us, his mouth-organ slotted into a jacket pocket. Their ages became irrelevant as they made their Highland music together afresh, Duncan accompanying Tom and Niellachan on his chanter, but with a break now and again for Gaelic songs from Hugh or Tom and a blether with whoever; and if the three MacCallum brothers didn't themselves play musical instruments or budge much from their preferred positions at the bar, it was still abundantly clear that they were as happy with the cultural offering as the rest of us, albeit that it was an ingrained and familiar part of their upbringing and island world, one to which we came as strangers but were quickly coming to know and like, and were growing ever more intrigued by.

Another thing we noticed back in Carsaig, as we feasted daily on the normally stunning view south across the sea to the neighbouring islands, with the Caledonian MacBrayne's steamer, the *King George V*, ploughing its languid and elegant furrow in the foreground as it circled Mull with its boatload of summer visitors to the smaller islands of Iona and Staffa, was that while Mull would all too frequently be experiencing a shower or downpour, there would be low-lying Colonsay basking unconcernedly in the sunshine as the clouds leapfrogged over it or ignored it altogether, preferring the high hills of the big islands or the Argyllshire mainland upon which to relieve themselves of their copious and soggy loads.

We joked about it, we were curious about it but thought little more of it at the time. The penny would not drop till after we had both finished our summer season jobs and left our Carsaig idyll behind us. It certainly hadn't yet dropped when Alasdair and Julia managed to get hold of director Michael Powell's 1945 black-and-white film, *I Know Where I'm Going*, which they showed in the dining room one late summer evening to guests, staff and invited locals. The film had been largely shot in Carsaig, much of it by the then unchanged granite pier from which Alasdair and I went out each day in the boat to set and lift his lobster creels. Key scenes had been filmed in the self-same boatshed now used by father and son Tom and Sandy Brunton, who shared the pier with us and fished in their coble for salmon which they trapped and lifted using bag nets set along the shore past the Nun's Cave. The island of 'Kiloran' to which the heroine, played by Wendy Hiller, has such a frustrating time trying to get across is, in reality, Colonsay.

Perhaps more influential, in a subliminal way, on my eventual determination to try to go and live on Colonsay with Jane, was the beautiful old ballad used as the film score. It begins 'I know where I'm going and I know who's going with me . . . '. When I was a small boy growing up in an isolated West Berkshire farmhouse, my mother used to sing it to me at my bedside, wistfully, heartbreakingly. It was so haunting I could hardly bear – or resist – listening to it, then or now. It evoked strange and powerful echoes, perhaps from another life or a life yet to come.

It is less fanciful to say that when we left Carsaig, after our long, sweet summer idyll had ended and autumn days had drawn in, we did not yet know that Jane was pregnant, that we would even live together let alone get married, or what direction our lives would take. In fact we were to marry in March 1972, and our first son, Daniel, was born less than three months later. 'I know where I'm going'? Neither of us, at that point in time, had a clue, though it wasn't too long before we started to find out.

By that Christmas, we had found a decent flat together not too far from Edinburgh's Haymarket, where we would await the arrival of our first-born. While I had been down south receiving characteristically generous hospitality – but also an understandable version of the 'third degree' – from Jane's parents, their family friend and doctor had spelt out my new responsibilities to me in terms which any five-year-old, even one who preferred engaging with clay, could not have failed to take on board. Jane's confinement, he made absolutely clear, would have to be spent where the best prenatal care would be available at all times in case any complications arose and not, most certainly not, in some rural backwater, for example a remote Hebridean island where such civilised requirements could not be entirely guaranteed.

However, the good doctor deemed Edinburgh acceptable and as well as working in the 'Ceramic Workshop' near the Castle I took the first steps in exploring the idea of getting us back to an island life, finding a cottage to live in, setting up a studio pottery and, I trusted, living happily ever after. It all seemed so simple to my innocent mind, and it was equally obvious which Hebridean island would be top of the shortlist – Colonsay – because it had always seemed to beckon, albeit that the fixation had been formed long-distance without any reality check. So, to begin to put this right I wrote to the island's sole proprietor and laird, Lord Strathcona, sketching out my aspirations and wondering whether he might have a cottage for us to live in and an old building for me in which to set up my pottery. To my delight I received an encouraging reply from his then wife, another Jane, who invited me over to the island for a recce.

Thus it was, though it was only a year since I had caught my first bedazzled but long-distance glimpse, that after a slow and bewitching ferry journey from West Loch Tarbert on the Mull of Kintyre mainland via the ports of call of Craighouse on Jura and Port Askaig on Islay, I walked, full of nervous excitement, down the gangplank of the M.V. *Arran* and set foot for the very first time on Colonsay's bustling pier.

Local eyes were always keen to see who was coming off the ferry and doubtless I was clocked by all those present as an unfamiliar summer season 'visitor' – the native islanders' preferred description, rather than the more disparaging 'tourist' – their choice of word, I would later come to appreciate, a true reflection of the courtesy and consideration they would invariably show any stranger who landed on their shores. Not that they were lacking in curiosity, but the usual Hebridean approach, I came to understand, was to engage the newcomer in the friendliest kind of conversation and to elicit information so agreeably and painlessly that the provider was usually completely unaware just how much they had parted with. The fact that this complete stranger had been met and greeted so warmly on the pier by Lady Jane Strathcona had not gone unnoticed, but the questions arising would soon enough be answered by the islanders' tried and trusted intelligence-gathering methods. By the time the ferry returned, usually two or three days later on its next round trip to the island, most details about the visitor and the purpose of his visit would either have been discovered directly or more or less accurately deduced from assorted clues, the results shared and compared and a perfectly newsworthy and generally reliable story about the stranger and his business would have been pieced together and steadily improved by general circulation.

The island Lady Jane showed me round exceeded all my imagined expectations. Even though I had gained some familiarity with the range and the splendour of Hebridean charms during the time spent on Mull, it was very surprising to find such variety within Colonsay's much more limited confines. The rocky and rugged east side of the island, with its 'capital' of Scalasaig, where the ferry berthed and the island's only shop, hotel and pub were located, was matched on the west by a huge expanse of soft green machair land, white sandy beaches, dark sea-beaten skerries and a huge, blue-grey, pulsating ocean stretching out to the extended line of the distant, western horizon, interrupted only by the lonely *Dubh Hirteach* ('The dark St Kildan') lighthouse.

Further on, a patchwork of neat, white croft-houses and small fields soon began to appear and in the very middle of the island there was a sheltered valley cradling a long, narrow and picturesque loch. Much more unexpectedly, there were substantial areas of broad-leafed woodland around the Strathcona mansion, Colonsay House, which lies between the Home Farm at Kiloran – so that's where 'Kiloran' came from – and one of the most beautiful bays anywhere on Earth, the golden-sanded, dune-fringed arc of douce Kiloran Bay which, for some reason, the *National Geographic Magazine* once accorded only second place in its world-wide assessment.

My memory tells me that the air was sweet and full of bird song, there were wild flowers everywhere, the cattle and sheep were fat and contented, that everyone and anyone who passed you on the road would give a cheery wave and were just as friendly if you got a chance to say hello. Moreover, there were tantalising glimpses of a different and fascinating community life going on – there was a lot of Gaelic being spoken, noticeably more than in the Ross of Mull, and tractors and trailers as well as cars buzzed by on the single-track roads. There also seemed to be a good few working boats using the harbour at Scalasaig, there were island children, there was chatter and banter, there was humour and laughter.

By the time Lady Jane had shown me a vacant and lovely old-fashioned cottage next to the pier and harbour that we might be able to live in and an old stone-built, slate-roofed boathouse to the side of the harbour in which I could set up my studio (subject to Lord Strathcona's approval, Lady Jane stressed, but with an optimistic look in her eye). I was hooked. Colonsay was perfect: when could we come?

It took another few frustrating months before the agreements were reached about the cottage and the boathouse, and the essential arrangements could be made for our move to the island. True to the all-you-need-is-love, who-cares-about-the-lack-of-ready-cash spirit of the age we were signed-up members of, we had little money to spend but didn't worry too much. We went to look for some furniture for our first unfurnished home together at Madame Doubtfire's junk-shop in Stockbridge, a veritable treasure trove. The biggest treasure turned out to be Madame Doubtfire herself who, weighing us up in an instant and reminding us that we would need a good kitchen table, pointed out and sold us a beautiful, big solid oak one for just one pound – a generous-hearted gesture if ever there was one. This was the same table under which our children crawled and scrawled and upon which they ate, drew, played games, and eventually outgrew and left behind for continuing parental use.

The furniture-buying might be skimped – who needed a bedstead when a double mattress on some chipboard propped up on kiln bricks would do? – but furnishing the new pottery studio was a more serious matter requiring a business-like focus and a scary amount of capital, neither of which had exactly proved fortes of mine hitherto. Though the bank seemed happy enough to feed the end-of-term overdraft habit I had established when at art school, they recoiled at my 'business' proposition and wouldn't help unless some other financial guarantees could be provided.

To the rescue came a bold and ambitious new government agency, set up only a few years before to try to reverse the population loss and general decline of Britain's remotest corners, the Highlands and Islands Development Board or the HIDB, as it was popularly known. They promised me a grant of just over £1600 to get the business set up which, they also said, I wouldn't ever have to repay as long as I kept it going for a minimum of five years. It was a calculated gamble on their part, one of a great many which they boldly took over the years, some of which failed quietly, others more spectacularly, but most of which produced tangible benefits for the people and the communities they were intended to help. The fact that, despite my repeated pleas to them, their grant cheques only reached me and my bank account six months after I had taken out a loan and spent the money on equipping the studio, I now grudge them not. What the HIDB was able to do for all those like me, I would gradually come to appreciate as I became more and more involved in community development issues in the years to come, was truly far-seeing and influential in helping to make the Highlands and Islands of today so much more positive-minded, in thought and in deed, than it was then – a period still characterised by the historic self-doubt and negativity to which too many Highlanders and Islanders had, not without some justification, become prone.

I had self-doubt and negativity all of my own making to try to keep in check as my pal Frank and I drove the stuffed-full hired van through the late August night to get the 6 a.m. ferry to Colonsay from the pier on West Loch Tarbert. It didn't help that we were pulled over by the flashing blue light of an Argyllshire police car in the wee small hours and asked to account for ourselves and our load but, in one of the many lessons I would come to learn about the Highland way of life and its sense of close community, it turned out that one of the policemen was a native of Carsaig and since I had got to know his father, Tom, and much more importantly since his father knew me, he knew too, because his neighbours Alasdair and Julia had naturally told old Tom, nearly as much about our Colonsay plans as we knew ourselves. We had authenticated our credentials and were sent on our way with wishes of good luck. We made as quick a round trip to Colonsay as ferry timetables then allowed to unload all the pottery equipment in the boathouse and, much more importantly, to get the cottage ready to live in so that I could bring my new family over to it on the next available ferry.

The *Arran* was a modern for its times, side-loading vehicular ferry – cars were parked in the hold of the vessel and driven onto a platform which hoisted you slowly to quayside level where you waited for a side flap, known as the ramp, to be lowered and over which you then drove onto the pier and away. The lift on the old *Arran* was notoriously temperamental: if the weight of vehicles wasn't distributed evenly on the ascending platform then it would stall mid-journey, have to be lowered back to hold level and the weight re-trimmed before you could try the whole thing all over again, sometimes more than once, before a successful disembarkation could be achieved. Patience, which I have in restricted quantities, was required as Jane, Daniel and I waited in our recently purchased first car, a fourth-hand, faded fawn Hillman Minx, price £65, number plate WSF 943, to emerge from the ship's hold, keeping fingers crossed while the hoist made its snail's-pace and worryingly noisy upward journey and the ramp was finally and all too slowly lowered onto the pier.

All eyes seemed to be upon us, the very newest and greenest of newcomers, as we drove the couple of hundred yards or so off the pier, past the old harbour, and parked the Hillman outside our new home. It seems unbelievable now but Jane was not only seeing it for the first time but had never even set foot on the island till this moment. Was it just that previous plans to visit together had been derailed by events or was it a symptom of that young and insecure man's tunnel vision which had resulted in such carelessness? In any event, Jane was as thrilled and excited to be there as the man who had led her there and who carried four-month-old Daniel, gurgling happily in his wicker basket, and then his mother over the threshold and into Glen Cottage. At least, that's what the diary I started two days later records, as it does that we were both bowled over by the beauty of the island as we drove right round it for the first time, and that all three of us slept deeply and soundly on our first night together in Colonsay's quiet and comforting embrace.

2

GETTING TO KNOW YOU

Our new home, Glen Cottage, seemed to welcome us with open arms. It had been built in 1881 by the island's carpenter and boat-builder, Alexander McNeill, to house his growing family, who had all lived and died there. It was a typical single storey 'but and ben' cottage; grey-slated roof, great thick walls of bright, whitewashed stone ending in a 'flying gable', two rooms downstairs and two small attic bedrooms upstairs, in which a full-grown adult could only stand upright directly under the roof ridge. These were accessed by a flight of time-worn and near vertical wooden steps that were more ladder than stairs and which our small children would come to use as a climbing frame when they weren't racing fearlessly up and down them. A much more recent flat-roof extension had been tacked onto one end to provide a kitchen, and a small room in the middle of the house, which had served for generations as the island's post office and telephone exchange, had been converted into a bathroom with a great, deep, old-fashioned bath in which one could wallow happily for hours.

There was a funny little black bakelite box with a revolving handle on one side which stood by the phone (telephone number 'Colonsay 46') on a hallway shelf: it was a magneto telephone and you had to wind the resistant handle in the box vigorously if you wanted to make a call because that was the way you generated the ringtone that attracted the attention of Flora (MacDougall but universally referred to as Flora Brown, her maiden name). Flora was a more than helpful lady, who from a room in her croft house in Kilchattan on the other side of the island operated the island's current telephone exchange and delivered a since unsurpassed twenty-four hour bilingual service which included the brilliant and entirely free supplement of finding out for you where the islander you were trying to get hold of was presently located, once Flora had ascertained for you that they weren't at home.

From our small living room, with its cosy open fire and super-efficient back boiler which heated the water, the cottage looked east onto the boathouse which the carpenter had used as his workshop and due west up the Scalasaig brae to the Church of Scotland church, two more semi-detached cottages and, to the right of the road, the island's one and only hotel and bar. It was probably due to all the timber which the carpenter had, no doubt carefully and lovingly, put into its construction, but the cottage smelt as well as felt good – a smell that was never more evocative than when one gratefully crossed its threshold again after returning home from a trip away to the mainland.

There was plenty to be getting on with. I had a stand at the HIDB's first ever Annual Craft Trade Fair, just seven weeks away in Aviemore, at which to show my own first 'Colonsay Pottery' pots and I hadn't even started to build the kiln yet. There was a nest to build too inside Glen Cottage, and there was an island full of islanders to get to know, all 128 of them, which is a lot when you haven't yet met any of them. The islanders, whom Neil Munro's peerless character Para Handy had once maligned in a reference to their exceptionally fine whelks – 'but the people iss so slow they cannot catch them' – were anything but. Our immediate next door neighbour, Finlay MacFadyen, who worked for Colonsay Estate, called round on our very first evening to see if we needed anything and, as well as lending some tools I had mentioned, there waiting for us next morning outside the back door was also a bag of coal which Finlay had found was now surplus to the Estate's holiday home requirements. There too was a box of fresh eggs which someone else – we had no idea who – had left for us. These were just the first of the countless acts of kindness which the good people of

Colonsay showed the Alexander family over the coming days and years, which characterised their way of life and changed our own for the better.

While Jane and Danny in his period-piece pram were quickly making friends wherever they went, I had to put my head down and get my pottery studio up and running. But there was no need to feel isolated because, out of friendly curiosity, more and more of the male islanders, young, old and in-between, started coming down to the ex-boathouse to say hello and see what this strange newcomer, the so-called 'potter', was up to. Finlay's youngest son, 'wee' Finlay, was my first and most assiduous visitor and he would come down to inspect my kiln-building and shelf-making progress just as soon as he climbed off the primary school bus each afternoon and he was, without fail, cheerily direct in letting me know how much or how little I had really achieved. My rate of progress varied, it could not be denied, with the number and nature of the distractions I gave into during the day. There were so many: the view across the sea from the door of the pottery, as far as Ben Cruachan and even snow-capped Ben Nevis over 60 miles away on the mainland on an exceptionally clear day, plus the comings and goings of the locals to the pier and harbour as well as those of the shore birds whose territory I now shared and was also getting to know.

But the biggest distraction of all came from some of the more senior male Gaels, who on gravitating, as sea-going islanders are accustomed to do, towards the natural hub of the pier and harbour to check out the state of the tide and what the local fishermen were doing, became increasingly inclined to see what the potter was up to and share the time of the day. 'The potter', for so he quickly became called – 'Well, Potter, what are you busy at this weather?' – was not just a bit of curiosity; he was clearly a harmless young fellow who had much to learn but was agreeably happy to listen. And listen he did, not infrequently spellbound, as they informed, entertained and generally riveted their new and highly receptive audience with their keenly observed and consistently humour-laced stories, which presented the many facets and idiosyncrasies of the island and its cast of islanders, both present and past. It was storytelling of an astonishing fluency and listenability: it was, I came to appreciate, an art form which the culture of the Gael had brought to near perfection after hundreds if not thousands of years of practice, and all you had to do was tune in properly, laugh enthusiastically and encouragingly (never a problem), maybe ask the odd question by way of further clarification, and soak it all up – my own lack of accomplishment not being taken amiss by the main conversationalists who did not seem to mind not having their natural flow interrupted.

No greater conversationalist was to be found on the island than *Para Mor*, 'Big Peter', as he was interchangeably known – Peter MacAllister, native *'Colosach'* of fishermen stock, ex-sailor and bosun in the Merchant Navy who had worked his way round the ports of the world on cargo boats and who now made his living fishing lobsters on the wild south-west side of Colonsay and, when back on dry land, serving as the island's telephone engineer and piermaster. Shyly at first, but very soon on a regular and daily basis, usually after he had done his initial telephone engineering job check-ups at the GPO 'radio station' and then collected the milk from Scalasaig Farm for various aunts and uncles as well as his own immediate family, Peter would call in at the pottery to say hello and share news and views on the life of the island and the wider world beyond, about both of which he was remarkably well informed.

It was Big Peter who, one still autumn day, first brought home to me the truly mesmerising nature of the native Gael's conversational power. He hadn't called in that morning but arrived down at the pottery mid-afternoon as the autumn sun shone brightly and warmly and the conversation (his mostly) started to flow likewise; and so richly, interestingly and unfailingly entertainingly that I only became aware how much time had passed when, with a bit of a start, I came to and realised that the sun had long since disappeared, the tide had filled the previously well-ebbed harbour and was now reflecting a full harvest moon which had risen high into the starry sky. I realised that I was surprisingly hungry too and so, evidently, was Big Peter who said, 'Ach well, Potter, I suppose we'd better go and get the tea' and left to return home for his by then overdue evening meal ('the tea' as it was termed, never 'dinner', while 'supper' was what locals called the sometimes substantial snack you would take much later in the evening); while I made some hurried attempts to tidy up the work I had failed to finish so that I could go back to the cottage and do the same. It occurs to me now that island conversations – particularly those with Big Peter – never really ended but were more like instalments in a lifelong dialogue that would merely be temporarily adjourned until you could pick it up again somewhere in the general vicinity of where you had parked it earlier.

My other regulars – all equally natural-born storytellers in their own individual ways – were of an older generation, born in the first few years of the twentieth century: Para Mor's uncle, 'Old Peter' or 'Para Clocs', the Darroch brothers Ross and Neil, and 'Aldy' MacAllister, a first cousin of old Peter's. Their visits, their stories and their insights as well as those of my many other less frequent visitors, fed my hunger – as if my inner world depended upon it – to find out more about the island microcosm that was Colonsay. These regular visitors of mine, good friends as they soon became, had kindled my fascination with their world which seemed so much richer and deeper-rooted than my own. As a consequence, though I did not properly appreciate what they were doing for me at the time, they had also sparked something in me and awoken an underused capacity for a little bit of useful self-improvement as I began to develop and pursue new interests that helped me to grow in both my knowledge of the island and my wider understandings. How fortunate I was to have landed in such a well-placed work spot which could not fail to attract passing visitors, not just the casual or regular holidaymakers who might be looking for a pot to take home but, in particular, the locals, who were inclined to call in on their way to or from the pier, shop and post office, to take a breather on the upturned wooden beer crate, which had been donated by one of my regular visitors to serve as a seat, and share their stories and reflections with me. And in Colonsay, I had learnt, there was a story for absolutely everything – even, it turned out, my old beer crate.

Hughie MacDougall, Flora at the telephone exchange's husband, had an artificial leg and a small, three-wheeler invalid car to go with it, a vehicle which could just about take one passenger but was sometimes commandeered to squeeze in a few extras when island hospitality required it. On one such overloaded mission a wheel had buckled and given way when, after scorching down the Hotel brae somewhere in excess of twenty-five miles an hour, it had developed a severe list followed by a terminal wobble while trying to negotiate the right-angled bend nearest the harbour, leaving the three-wheeler and its complement with no choice but to abandon their now capsized vessel, manhandle it onto the verge and reformulate their travel plans. And there it stayed for several weeks, propped up on a beer crate – Hughie worked part-time at the Hotel – after the wheel had been removed for despatch via the ferry to the mainland for official examination and a promised replacement. Then one morning and many weeks later the three-wheeler had gone but the beer crate remained, now welded to the soft verge – though not for long, as Big Peter, who had long since made his assessment of its potential, carried the beer crate down to the pottery on one of his visits with more than a glint of satisfaction and a '*Seo, a ph?tter* (Here, o potter), you've been needing this for a long time', before taking the weight off his feet and pressing it, for the first of numberless occasions, into what proved to be invaluable and long-lasting service.

One of my newly kindled interests was in local history, brought vividly to life by my regulars. *Riasg Buidhe* (roughly pronounced 'Rask Boo-ie' and meaning 'Yellow Marsh') featured often in their stories because Aldy and Old Peter had spent their formative years there, as had several other then resident islanders whom I also got to know; and Big Peter's own MacAllister father, uncles, aunts and cousins had all grown up there. They were all steeped in the stories of this unique Colonsay community.

Riasg Buidhe, a deserted fishing village, lies a couple of miles up the coast from the Scalasaig Pier and just over the hill that sits behind the present day settlement at Glassard and it comprised a St Kilda-like row of eight terraced cottages plus three more detached ones. There are also remains of an ancient chapel and a tiny graveyard containing a headstone with a keyhole in it – the story my visitors told being that if you find the key you can unlock it and go straight to heaven – and where once had stood an ancient and wonderfully carved cross depicting the bearded, chubby-cheeked head of some surely much-loved saint, until it was taken away to keep an eye on St Oran's Well by present-day Colonsay House in another part of the island, Kiloran. The village appears to get its name from the sea of yellow irises that in springtime covers the boggy ground lying between the gently inclining village street and the small natural harbour on the rocky shore called *Port a Bhàta* (pronounced 'Port-uh Vah-tuh' and meaning Boat Harbour) where the Riasg Buidhe fishermen used to keep their boats.

Though every cottage had a small piece of croft ground, enough to keep a cow and grow some potatoes and corn, the community that lived here made its living from the surrounding sea. The four or five boats that fished out of Riasg Buidhe when Old Peter was a boy each had a crew of three or four and they normally began their season at the end of February by fishing for cod. They would set their long lines, with an average of two hundred hooks each, all baited with a dog whelk, in the deep water north of Colonsay where the Atlantic Ocean has by then rolled in thousands of uninterrupted miles from the icy coast of Labrador. The men would start their cod fishing season near the awe-inspiring Gulf of Corryvreckan whirlpool at the north end of Jura, so memorably filmed in *I Know Where I'm Going*, and would move their lines gradually further and further westward, following the cod, until they reached a point several miles west of Colonsay in May. The lines were lifted and reset every day, and as many as 150 cod could be taken from a single line on a single lift by this method. The fishermen gutted and cleaned the fish and brought them home to Riasg Buidhe where they were salted in barrels for several weeks. The pickled cod were then dried on the rocks in the open air before being tied into bales which were then taken to be sold in Greenock by the *Dunara Castle* – the nostalgically recollected steamer that ferried cargo and passengers from the Broomielaw in Glasgow through the Inner to Outer Hebrides and back on a twice-weekly basis for the astonishing period of nearly seventy years until the late 1940s.

After the cod-fishing had come to an end the lobster-fishing would commence and the Riasg Buidhe fishermen used to spend their summer months working the wild western shoreline of Jura which lay visible opposite their homes some eight miles away across the sea. The fishermen camped each night in one or other of the many big caves behind the 'raised beaches' which dot that deserted shore, returning home at weekends with their catch which, Old Peter recalled, was often twenty dozen lobsters from forty creels which were usually lifted twice a day. The older male children, Old Peter amongst them, used to spend the week with the men and gather winkles from the shore for which they were paid half a crown a bushel, eight bushels (about four hundredweights) being gathered on a decent spring-tide ebb, and which eventually made their way with the lobsters to the mainland markets. The southern coast of the Ross of Mull was similarly worked for lobsters by the Riasg Buidhe and other Colonsay fishermen, and it was not unheard of in those days, when the boats relied entirely on a square sail, with a set of long oars called 'sweeps' in reserve, for the men to have to row them the ten or sometimes twenty miles back to Colonsay when the wind was not favourable for sailing.

The lobster creels were usually baited with mackerel when in season or with the more year-round, reliable saithe or lithe which, unlike the posher forms of whitefish with which Colonsay seas once abounded, had always managed to withstand the raids by Scottish east coast trawlers which were roundly blamed by Colonsay fishermen for their depredation of a formerly productive and reliable local fishing harvest. The '*piocach*' (pew-kuch) as the saithe/lithe was called by everyone on Colonsay, whether English or Gaelic speaker, was readily enough caught at one or other of the many offshore fishing stations – small areas above particularly nutrient-rich parts of the seabed where fish habitually fed. At sea these were traditionally located with pinpoint accuracy by lining up two island landmarks, such as the top of an iron age fort as it just appeared from behind a certain hill; and all had names such as '*Roc Dhun Eibhinn*', 'the fishing station of (with a sightline of) Edwin's Fort'. A hand-held line of strong twine, with a chunky lead weight on the bottom to let you know when you have hit the seabed, and a set of half a dozen hooks with feathers attached, called 'darrows', is then rhythmically lowered and raised and the fish, if they are there at all, will usually chase the feather and become hooked – often several at a time if conditions are right.

Come the autumn the young of the piocach, called 'cuddies', meander close into the shore, hugging the faces of the rock where the sea meets the land. Cuddies are a delicacy – delicious fried in flour – that were also part of the staple diet of home-caught or home-grown fare that generations of Colonsay folk had been raised on. Each part had its natural season and place in the age-old routine of the community, although the inevitable changes to the local way of life meant that some once-cherished traditions were being abandoned.

Not completely, insofar as the cuddy-fishing was concerned, I discovered when I looked out from the pottery on one of those tranquil, late September afternoons when the sun shone endlessly. The air was warm and still and the sea, at its most benign, was filling the harbour noiselessly and almost surreptitiously. I was bemused to see that, despite the fact that no ferry was due for at least another twenty-four hours, several of the older native Colosachs were gathering and taking up positions at various points along the harbour wall and slipway with the intention, so it quickly became clear, of catching some fish. As well as Aldy, Neil, Ross and Big Peter, there too was Mary Clark who lived by the church in a cottage that had once been Scalasaig Primary School when, before the First World War, the island still needed two, one for each side of the island, and who had for many years helped her late brother David run Colonsay Hotel. There too was Aldy's neighbour, Clarence MacIntyre, whose unusual Christian name made him no less of a pedigree Gael. Old Peter had arrived as well to play a support role and Jasper, the roadman, was clearly also in the know and was just pulling up in his faded turquoise A40, clearly intent on joining what must have been a pre-arranged gathering.

The snatches of lively chatter that drifted my way across the harbour were all in Gaelic, that strange, breathful and musical language that I knew I really wanted to understand, even though I did not yet appreciate the difficulty I would have in doing so. I decided to wander round to see what was going on and, with that characteristic gentle courtesy, which would nevertheless come to frustrate me deeply as my efforts to acquire their alluring but elusive tongue proceeded in the months and years ahead, they had all switched seamlessly to using English by the time I had arrived so that I would not feel left out of their conversation.

Everyone present, except Old Peter, whose eyesight was now not quite up to the task, and myself had a short home-made hazel rod with a bit of line attached and a single hook at the end with a winkle on it, one of a small heap that each had previously gathered and cooked, extracting the winkle from its shell on the quayside with a bent safety pin or somesuch.

Each also had some cold, boiled potatoes to hand or was grinding up some of their pile of winkles on the harbour's granite blocks. The resulting mash was thrown into the sea to draw in the swarming cuddies and the baited hook was then lowered into the midst of the gathered fish, one of which would investigate the winkle and, hopefully, take a last bite before being hooked, hoicked and landed by the alert fisherman or woman. It was good fun to watch, even more to do and was made even more agreeable by the companionable blether and humour-laced competition of the various anglers. I learnt too that this was called *carraig* (pronounced 'Ka-regg' and meaning a fishing rock) fishing and that there were many carraigs around the shores of Colonsay and Oronsay which were easily identified by the sizeable bowl-like holes found in the fishing stances which, typically, are small promontories of rock which stick out a bit from the shore line and usually have near-vertical rockfaces so that you can readily see and catch the cuddies below. The holes had been created over successive generations by islanders grinding their limpets, whelks and similar into the bait then used to lure the cuddies and sometimes bigger fish. From the slipway Neil and Ross pointed out two more stances along the rocky shore to the lighthouse, *Carraig Dhonnachaidh an Òir* and *Carraig Ghilleasbuig Ruadh*, 'Duncan of the Gold's fishing rock' and 'Red-headed Archibald's fishing rock', which they might well use if the sea and wind conditions suited those stances better. And when I popped up later to the island shop and post office in Glassard to get some petrol from my neighbour Finlay's brother, Big Angus, I saw that three of Old Peter's Riasg Buidhe born and bred older sisters, Old Katie – the last person then living to have been educated at Scalasaig Primary School before it was closed – Effie and Maggie, were also fishing from below the Manse at *Carraig Port a' Mhinisteir,* 'The fishing rock of the Minister's harbour'.

None of the carraig fishers that day went home without having happily revisited their younger days and secured a good feed of cuddies as well although, it later transpired, Aldy had paid more heavily for his catch than anyone else. He used another traditional method of mash-baiting that involved chewing up a cold boiled potato and spitting the results onto the sea below – a technique which had the merit of spraying a notably fine mash over a surprisingly large surface area provided the expulsive force used was sufficient. This was Aldy's undoing for, after one blast too many, the bottom set of his false teeth had also been given a jet-propelled launch to join the bits of carefully masticated potato in their parabolic final flight to a watery grave, there being no fish big or bold enough, so it appeared, to take much more than a passing interest in the grinning denture as it sank menacingly but inexorably to the harbour floor. Aldy had been fishing on his own after everyone else had gone home when this unfortunate accident took place and I only found out about it because I had noticed – gazing out from the pottery door next day, when I should have been working hard at my potter's wheel – that there he was on his hands and knees, evidently engaged, so I enthusiastically assumed, in pursuing some other fascinating traditional aspect of Colonsay life about which I knew nothing but simply had to try and find out more. He shared the plain truth of the situation with me and we hunted hard together both then and at low water again the next day, though the denture could not be found. It was several years later, after Aldy had passed on, that while I was doing some work on the skeg of my own boat in the very same corner of the harbour a funny pinkish-greenish glint of something unusual in a gap at the bottom of the harbour wall caught my eye. It just had to be Aldy's bottom set, and although I wasn't sure whether to laugh or to cry I steeled myself to the task, extricated them with a pair of pliers and, gripping them tightly, climbed up the harbour steps, legged it to the very end of a thankfully deserted pier and re-buried them at sea, with a silent but fervent prayer that they would never again put in another unsettling appearance.

3

LEARNING THE LANGUAGE

Though I never did manage to master the Gaelic language or the unique south Argyllshire dialect that was spoken on Colonsay and Oronsay I derived some rich rewards, as well as the odd headache, for my efforts over the years. As a consequence, I came that bit closer to understanding the place and its people than I would have done by restricting myself to the sole medium of *beurla cruaidh* – 'hard English' – the Gaels' description of a tongue which they considered lacked the softness and subtlety of inference and sound which their own had in such musical and mysterious abundance.

Colonsay Gaelic was the very much alive, first and preferred language used constantly by at least 70 of the island's 128 permanent residents when we started living there in the late summer of 1972. That it was not spoken, though pretty well fluently understood, by most of the other islanders was a symptom of its gradual and apparently unstoppable decline as the island's predominant language, which it had been for many hundreds of years up till then. Most, though with some exceptions, of the children of Gaelic-speaking parents would usually only respond to them in English, even in the privacy of their own homes and even though they understood every Gaelic word that was spoken to them.

Gaelic had ceased to be the predominant language of the playground in the 1950s and it hadn't been taught or given any place at all in the school curriculum for generations. The attitude of central and local government was one of uninterested neglect at best; and the dominant language of the 'modern world', of television and radio and of all the visitors, except the diaspora formed by the good number of older native islanders who had moved away but still came back regularly to the island to visit relatives, was English. Is it any wonder, then, that the local Gaelic speakers themselves had an ambivalent attitude towards their native tongue which was faithfully reflected back to me when I boldly announced to some of my regular visitors to the pottery that I was keen to try and learn the language. 'What do you want to learn Gaelic for, Potter, it's no bloody use to anyone today!' 'Well, *you* wouldn't have got very far without it,' came the instant riposte to his question from another Gael who was standing alongside him. Their shared view appeared to be that though they were quietly pleased I was taking an interest in their native tongue, they saw it as little more than just another sign of the young enthusiast's harmless eccentricity which, with their customary forbearance, they were only too happy to accommodate – as long as it did not actually require them to converse slowly and painfully with the oh-so-painful-ly-slow language learner and thereby interrupt the normal and agreeable flow of an otherwise perfectly good conversation in their other language – English – in which they were also com-pellingly, irresistibly, fluent.

So how, then, was I to find a way forward? The *Teach Yourself Gaelic* book wouldn't teach me the living south Argyllshire dialect of the language as it was spoken on Colonsay, nor would Gaelic programmes on the radio, then confined to just fifteen minutes of Fred MacAulay introducing and playing Gaelic records every weekday lunchtime backed up by a heavy-duty Gaelic service, *Deanamaid Aoradh* ('Let us worship'), then broadcast every Sunday afternoon, which only compounded my feelings of gloom. I would have to find a teacher amongst the islanders. Successive natives made their excuses, but Aldy volunteered cheerfully for the task, and most Wednesday evenings during the long months of winter, I would make my way up the hill from Glen Cottage past the Hotel and into the only detached house in neighbouring 'Squint Street', *a srathaid chaim*, where Aldy lived with his wife Jessie, known locally as 'Jessie Aldy'.

With a '*Thig a stigh, a Photter*' (heek-uh sty, uh fotter) which translates literally as 'come thou inside, o Potter' I would be welcomed into the house and, before I was seated in front of the Rayburn, Jessie Aldy would have poured me a cup of tea – '*Ghabh thu copan ti, a Photter*' (Ga oo kop-un tee), 'you'll take a cup of tea, o Potter' – that was proffered with such immediate and unwavering Hebridean hospitality that it would have been impossible to refuse, although experience suggested that if you could find a way you might be better to. I never found one and so had to get used to experiencing the strongest tea I had ever tasted, before or since – tea that started its life in its metal teapot quite unexceptionably at breakfast time but was then revived on a regular basis throughout the day by the addition of more tea and enough water to ensure the pot kept permanently on the baking hot hob was always full, gently simmering away and ever ready for hospitable action. The result come the evening was a brew of such well-stewed ferocity that it would feel as if the enamel on your teeth had been subjected to a fairly serious galvanic experience, albeit that the intensified caffeine content must surely have helped my concentration.

Concentration was needed on a number of counts. Aldy was a very intelligent and interesting man, but neither of us had been trained as a teacher and so we made the lesson up as we went along and as best we could: one of us would offer a phrase, Aldy would give me the Colonsay Gaelic version, we would then endeavour, not always successfully, to break it down into its component parts and I would try and repeat it and then write it down phonetically in my notebook for some later revision.

The first thing I had to get acclimatised to was that the dialect of Gaelic spoken on Colonsay and Oronsay was markedly different in some aspects from the language spoken by the great majority of Gaels who lived in or came from the Gaelic-speaking areas to the north, and whose version of it had long since become enshrined as the received orthodoxy in 'Teach Yourself Gaelic' books and the like, which I had enthusiastically acquired. It wasn't just that in Colonsay, as in Islay to the south, the 'a' sound in many

Gaelic words (as in 'man') was often flattened into an 'eh' sound (as in 'men') but that some other key sounds had evolved quite differently in the dominant northern version of Gaelic, despite the recognition which the written version of the language gave to the authenticity of the southern Argyllshire pronunciation. So, for example, the word for 'summer' is spelt *'samhradh'* in Gaelic and its pronunciation in 'received' Gaelic sounds akin to 'sow-ruh'. But in Colonsay Gaelic it sounds more like 'sevver-ug' because the first 'a' is flattened, the 'mh' is still a 'v' sound in the way that it is written rather than the spoken 'w' sound and, similarly, the final 'dh' is closer to the final 'g' sound in the word 'glug' than the more aspirated version used further north.

My struggle to get to first base with the language was not made any easier by something called 'aspiration', which made the sounds of words change so radically that they more often that not slipped and slid out of earshot like passing breaths of wind. I got used to some of the easier aspirations – for example the 'b' sound becoming a 'v' sound when a possessive pronoun was put in the front of the word, e.g. *'am bàta'*, um bah-tuh, the boat, became *'mo bhàta'*, mo vah-tuh, my boat. But nouns starting with c, f, g, s and t seemed to metamorphose into elusive, spectral shadows of their formerly substantive selves and would taunt and tease with a kind of catch-me-if-you-can quality, and even if you did catch and identify one of these fleeting phantoms it was at the expense of failing to understand the cataract of words which had cascaded past you in the meantime.

In any case the 'lesson' was always more of a gossipy conversation about island life and its goings-on, interspersed with snippets of some useful Gaelic instruction, plus frequent interjections from Jessie Aldy who would not hesitate to pass comment on some phrase that Aldy and I had conjured up, in all tutorial innocence, for translation. Thus, my phonetic 'Potter's Gaelic Primer and Phrasebook' which I started to compose from my notes into a blue school exercise book after each lesson, faithfully records this example of our tripartite collaboration: *golluv um meenishter uh gurting coo,* 'the Minister went away (on the ferry) to get a dog', *ach bee-ich un coo na hootcherkoog yeh,* 'but the dog will be company for him', which Jessie finished off with a quickfire *buh-chor a ga ben urting,* 'he should get a wife'. Occasionally Aldy would instinctively, though unwisely, choose to parry a remark from Jessie and provoke a period of volley and return which usually ended in a score draw and a graceful change of subject; 'Ach, you'll take a scone, Potter, and another cup of tea.'

'A scone would be lovely, thank you Jessie, but I'm fine for tea just now.'

Aldy and Jessie passed away within a few months of each other in 1975, leaving the remaining residents with fond memories and a slow learner without a tutor. Aldy's neighbour, Neil Darroch, always liked a challenge and agreed to take me on, and many an enjoyable evening I spent with him and his brother, Ross, who lived next door and who would usually come and join us for the 'craic'. Though the Gaelic tuition was fairly minimal, the entertainment and wider educational value of the brothers' conversation was invariably maximal.

Bit by slowly absorbed bit my knowledge of this ancient and intriguing language (which Aldy assured me had been spoken by Adam and Eve in the Garden of Eden and was therefore understood by all animals, but which to me was so different from the standard European languages I had been exposed to in school), improved and my regular visitors would at least often greet me in the language: 'Well, *a Photter, de mar a tha thu an diugh?*' (Well, o Potter, how art thou today?), and I would usually give them one of the cheekier of the traditionally Colonsay responses Aldy was responsible for teaching me: *'Tha mi gu diollaidh maith, gu'n robh maith mór agad'* (I'm devilish well, it was good of you to ask). And when two or more happened to be visiting at the same time they would sometimes speak Gaelic to each other, expecting me to understand, particularly when the punchlines of a good story would lose too much in translation, and they would always patiently explain something I had missed when I asked them, until eventually I began to miss less.

But even when you have understood the literal meaning, it

seems well-nigh impossible for an outsider to know what unique
subtleties of inherent extra meaning – for those in the know,
so to speak, of which you can never quite be one – seem to
be getting lost in translation or remain untranslatable. Andrew
('A.S.') McNeill, who farmed Oronsay and though not a native
Gaelic speaker was the son of one and well understood it and
the people it belonged to, used to say that the Gaels had several
languages, including dance and the various instrumental forms
of musical expression, not least classical bagpiping, 'pibroch', of
which he was a magisterial exponent. And yet the music in the
sounds and expression of the Gaelic words themselves also seem
to convey long-embedded layers of soulful meaning, never more
directly than when they are used to express the native Gael's love
and longing for the places and people to which they belong. An
example is the poem, *'S Fhada Thall Tha Mise*, Far from Home
I Am, written by Andrew's brother-in-law, Donald 'Garvard'
McNeill, while doing his National Service in England, a world
away from the island of his upbringing, Oronsay. The poem also
brings home just how vital the Gaelic language was to Donald's
sense of self, but it might also serve as an epitaph for the demise of
the ancient and expressive Gaelic language once universally spoken by the people of Colonsay and Oronsay, so pleasing to the
ear even when the literal meaning remained stubbornly elusive.

'S Fhada Thall Tha Mise

'S fhada, 's fhada thall tha mise,
'S fhada thall bhon eilean aluinn,
Eilean aluinn snamh 'san iar,
Ailleagan gu brath 'nam chridh,
's fhada, 's fhada thall tha mise.
Orasa nan traighean grinneal,
Traighean grinneal min nan sluaisreadh,
Stuadhantan ur bhu uchd a chuain,
Bualadh fuaimneach mar o chionn:
Orasa nan traighean grinneal.

'S'ann 'nad thamh a fhuair mi m'arach,
Fhuair mi 'm'arach òg is m'altrum,
Laithean samhraidh, maothach, blath,
Casrusigt' ruith mi taobh Loch Ban.
'S'ann 'nad thamh a fhuair mi m'arach
'S truagh an-diugh an Tir nan Gall mi,
Tir nan Gall is mi 'nam aonar,
Daoine coibhneil air gach taobh,
Ach 'se Beurla th'air gach beul.
'S truagh an-diugh an tir nan Gall mi.

'Far from Home I Am'

Far, so far away am I,
Far, so far my lovely isle,
Island swimming in the west,
Jewel in my heart for ever,
Far, so far, from you am I.
Oronsay, your sandy beaches,
Sands the seas have milled so fine,
Breakers born upon the ocean,
Crashing down, time after time,
On Oronsay's fine-sanded bays.

In your balm I did my growing,
Got my nurture, spent my childhood,
Soft, warm days of gentle summer
Running barefoot by the lochside.
Balm and comfort of my growing.
Today I'm in a foreign country,
All on my own, land of strangers,
Kindly folk are all around me
But it's English they're are all speaking:
A foreign land where I feel lonely.

In any case, I was as captivated listening to the older Colon-say Gaels' use of my native language as I was thoroughly challenged by trying to acquire theirs. To my ear, their English was more than fluent, it sounded and flowed better: clear as spring water, seemingly purified and refreshed by a subterranean Gaelic language filtration process before emerging into the daylight as a sparkling conversational stream. The *beurla cruaidh,* 'harsh English' that I spoke, they would never need to succumb to, and instead, they effortlessly transmogrified, softened and sweetened it to make it beguiling to the ear, as much for its music as its content.

The clarity of their diction too left BBC English in the shade, let alone most of its other variations. When I said 'when' it would emerge as an estuarine, totally aitchless and almost 'w'-free 'wen' with a dull, nasal emphasis on the 'en'; when old Ross Darroch said the word you could distinctly hear the 'w' sound begin as a soft 'ch' sound, as in 'loch', before being closely followed by the clear 'wuh' sound of the 'w' and then the breathy 'heh' sound of the 'h' – a combination which expanded and upgraded the duller-sounding standard English version. The word 'where', which received the same initial transformation, would be further enriched by the lovingly rolled 'errr' sound, and in a word like 'spring' the individual savour applied to each of the 's', 'p' and 'r' consonants gave such words their uniquely distinctive timbre and resonance and greater vigour. The Gael's predisposition to give the aitch sound its full value meant that simple, workaday words were given extra depth and texture; like the word 'deep' where the long vowel sound was extended and aspirated, somehow making it sound more pregnant with inherent meaning. It also meant that when it came to normally sloppy conjunctions of words like 'with him' you would invariably hear both aitches articulated precisely and separately whereas in my kind of English you would be lucky to hear one.

There was a more lilting, storyteller's cadence too to the delivery of the resulting sentences, an ebbing and a flowing of crescendos and decrescendos with frequent emphasis and expressive, sometimes explosive, relish applied to key words which, like punchlines within punchlines, drew you right into the story, even if it was one that, recounted in bog-standard English by a similar mainlander, might otherwise have left you cold.

When I listen again to the all too tiny handful of tape recordings I made of some of the older Scalasaig residents like Mary Clark, Morag Titterton (née MacAllister), Ross Darroch, Old Peter MacAllister and his sister Maggie, all born well before the start of the First World War, I am reminded of the impression their stories of their Colonsay lives made upon me, how much I was drawn to them as if they held a vital key to understanding my much less well grounded one. The context and narrative of their lives seemed so much more rooted and secure than my own, and I was always hungry for more. I loved listening to them.

There were also a few older Colonsay voices to be found, if not heard, in the written word, both prose and poems, and I looked eagerly to them too for further clues as to earlier versions of Colonsay life and lives. The prose-writer I turned and returned to most was *Murchadh Chalum,* Murdo McNeill, the son of *Calum* or Malcolm who was the Head Gardener of Colonsay Gardens. After training at Kew Gardens Murdo came back to manage the Gardens himself and compile his jewel of a reference book, published in 1910, *Colonsay, One of the Hebrides*: 'Its plants, their local names and uses – legends, ruins and place-names – Gaelic names of birds, fishes etc. – climate, geological formation, etc.' It is an authentic treasure trove, bringing the islanders' island of the late nineteenth century to richly detailed life with scholarly veracity guaranteed by its remarkable home-grown author. John De Vere Loder, who in 1935 produced his encyclopaedic reference work, *Colonsay and Oronsay in the Isles of Argyll*, which I also opened on an almost daily basis, pays generous tribute to Murdo: 'In all matters depending on local knowledge Mr Murdoch McNeill has been an invaluable collaborator. He knows the island and its lore better than anyone now living and has spent the greater part of his life in service to his native soil. His own book has been freely drawn upon wherever the same ground is covered.'

The other homegrown prose-writer I looked to was an equally remarkable islander but a lot harder going to read, partly because the book I had acquired, *The Prose Writings of Donald McKinnon*, was in very rich Gaelic, which took much slow and painful effort to decipher, and partly because his thirteen, very lengthy and densely-written essays published in *The Scotsman* during 1887 also required a magnifying glass to get to grips with, so small was the print on my photocopies. The author was still known in the 1970s by the name he had been given by his fellow islanders, *Domnhull Mhiogaras,* Donald from Miogaras – the name of the croft at the very northern end of the Kilchattan crofting area on the west side of the island where he grew up and which, at the time of his birth in 1839, had a population of around 250 – just over a quarter of the island's record-ever total of nearly a thousand. This Colonsay boy walked the length of Kilchattan each day to get his first schooling from an old but much-loved schoolmaster in what was little more than a stone-walled shack overlooking Port Mor, with its damp, earth floor, driftwood benches, slates to write on and a couple of holes in the leaky, thatched roof to help the smoke from the two peat fires find their way out of the building, but in due course he became the first-ever Professor of Celtic Studies at Edinburgh University in the 1880s. His vivid and affectionate essay about his early education, *'An Seann Sgoil'*, 'The Old School', shines a light on the character of the author every bit as much as it does on this illuminated sliver of Colonsay's past.

'The Professor', as he was more commonly referred to locally, went on to produce a series of scholarly and meticulously considered essays and articles in lucid but generally prosaic prose, in both Gaelic and English. They include rather too few, though always very revealing, shafts of light on the island way of life as it was, and increasingly became, as the dramatic population decline that took place over the course of the nineteenth century hit hard. Most of Colonsay's traditional crofting areas were turned by the then McNeill lairds into farms and their former crofting tenantries effectively pressured into emigrating, though not, it has to be said, with the ruthlessness of the notorious Sutherland Clearances. The Professor, who was, according to one of his students, the Reverend Donald Lamont, 'the most unassuming and unaffected, hospitable and genial of men' and a wonderfully patient, effective and, in his turn, much-loved teacher, had also become a pillar of the Edinburgh establishment; and as such not inclined by temperament or social position to parade his private thoughts in public.

However, in one of his *Scotsman* articles, the Colonsay boy eventually gave vent to his innermost feelings. The article, entitled 'Lonely Colonsay' extols the island's scenic attractions and historical connections and while, as Professor McKinnon of Edinburgh University, he does not forget to include a short paean of praise to Lord Colonsay, the island's McNeill laird and former Lord Advocate when Sir Robert Peel was Prime Minister, and his significant Estate improvements, as *Domnhull Miogaras* from Colonsay he concludes with the following *cri de coeur*:

> Apart from local feeling or sentiment, one cannot help having the conviction that in the social and economic conditions of the Hebrides are some facts and circumstances which the 'dismal science' finds it hard to explain. Speaking broadly, the southern (Hebridean) isles are suited for a numerous and substantial tenantry, the crown and glory of a countryside. Yet this class is disappearing year by year. From its isolated position, and its resources by land and sea, few places are better fitted to maintain a rural population than the island of Colonsay. And yet one cannot but observe the symptoms of 'passing away' on every hand. When a shoemaker dies there is no one to take his place. The wool is sent to the mills of Jedburgh and Inverness. The goodwife's spinning wheel is silent and the local weaver starves. Everything substantial

is sent south: everything, the shadowy and the substantial, returns from the south. A marriage is a rarer event than a Parliamentary election. This interesting island, fondly remembered by visitors and inexpressibly dear to those brought up in it, looks as if doomed to a solitude not due to its geographical position alone.

The Professor died on Christmas Day, 1914, in Balnahard Farmhouse in the north of the island, which he leased from Colonsay Estate and used as his second home when able to get away from his academic duties in Edinburgh. The farm was managed by Murchadh Chalum whose own book was proofread and corrected for him by the 70-year-old Professor.

The prose these two learned men have left behind is fascinating but it is the poems which more faithfully reflected the shared sensibility of Colonsay people, in particular their love of nature and their sense of humour. As my Gaelic language understanding grew, so too did my interest in the island's poetic heritage and, not least, in Colonsay's most fondly remembered poet, 'The Bard', whose songs – for in the oral tradition of the Gael most poems were composed to be sung – were still very much alive in the minds of the older generation of islanders.

A bard was a local poet who, I came to discover, composed perceptive and often very witty songs about the place and the people he or she knew intimately. In the pre-TV world the Gael had a veritable passion for making music and songs; songs for work, rowing a boat, singing a child to sleep, songs for every occasion. The gift of poetic composition in Gaelic-speaking communities was surprisingly common – surprising, at least, to one raised in an essentially urbanised culture dominated by the printed word – and it is recorded that during the nineteenth century well over thirty men and women, from just one small crofting township in the north Argyllshire island of Tiree, were known to have the gift of making songs.

Many different Colonsay people had also composed songs for a then very receptive local audience; most of which are now lost forever because they were transmitted orally. A few of them were saved because they were written down, and some fine examples may be found in the small but priceless collection brought together by Alastair MacNeill Scouller in his book *Moch is Anmoch* [Early and Late]: *The Gaelic poetry of Donald A. MacNeill* [aka 'Donald Garvard'] *and Other Colonsay Bards.* If someone had the gift of composing the occasional, often humorous song, they would be known 'as a bit of a bard', but the title 'the Bard' went to the community's most accomplished and respected practitioner and, in his day, this was Gilleasbuig MacNeill.

'The Bard' was born in 1843 into the self-reliant and vigorous fishing community of Riasg Buidhe, in whose traditions he was raised before spending many years away from Colonsay working in the Merchant Navy, in due course as Ship's Mate. He eventually came back to Riasg Buidhe to resume his old life of fisherman–cottar and occasional boat–builder, but now confirmed as both bachelor and bard. In his late seventies he moved over with the rest of the Riasg Buidhe folk to the new houses in Glassard, about which he composed the following, then still frequently quoted, song. It was addressed to Old Peter's sister, Maggie MacAllister, then a young woman, whom he had watched growing up in Riasg Buidhe and liked to tease.

Oran a Ghlais-aird

Theid thu null leam, a ruin
Bidh tigh ur again s'a Ghlais-aird
'S bhon than a h'aiteridh cho mor
Gheibh sinn oran 'san dol seachad
Chi thu fhein gu bheil iad riomhach
Air an gniomh le aol 's clachan
Sgleatan tana Bhaile-chaolais
Tha gan dion bho gaoith 's fhrasan
'S ged nam ballaichean cho ard,
A cumail sgath oirnn o'n gheallaidh

Learning the Language

Mun theid aca ruith o'n Mars
Gheibh sinn pairt dhe anns a Ghlaisaird
'S nuair a thoir sinn an rathad ur
Geibh sinn inneal-giulain dhachaidh
Cha n'iarr sinn each air son a shlaodach
S'e cho luath ri gaoith an earraich
Mar thu air son a dhol a cheilidh
Mar tha a dol a dhionnsaidh banais
'S'nuair a bhios tu dol d'on bhuth
Bheir e null fhein s'a leanabh
Theid thu null leam, a ruin
Bidh tigh ur againn s'a Ghlasaird
'S bhon na h-aiterich cho mor
Gheibh sinn oran s'an dol seachad

The Glassard Song

Come on over with me, sweetheart
A new place will be ours in Glassard
And the houses are so splendid
We'll have a song there in the passing
You'll see yourself that they are handsome
Well constructed, lime and stone
Good, thin slates from Ballachulish
Will shield us from wind and rain
And the walls they are so lofty
That you cannot even see the moon
But if a storm shall come from Mars★
We'll get some in Glassard soon
And since we got the new road in
We'll get a whining-engine home†
And it won't need a horse to pull it

★Taken by the locals to be a foretelling of the coming of radio
to the island
†The bard's description of the motor car

For it's as swift as springtime wind
And if you want to go a-calling,
Or maybe going to your wedding,
Or when you need to do the shopping
It will take you and the baby
Come on over with me, sweetheart,
A new place will be ours in Glassard
And the houses are so splendid
We'll have a song there in the passing.

Although the Bard never married it would seem that he had considered the implications and was simply biding his time waiting for the right person to come along.

An t-Achmhasan

Sin mar labhair Alasdair
'S e 'g radh gun robh mi gorach
Gun robh me fuasach aimeadeach
Bhi fantail ann am onar
Nam biodh seorsa bean agad
A bhiodh a 'fuireach comhla riut
Cha chuireadh fuachd no acras
O'n Shathurna gu Dhomhnaich
O! ni sinn faighidinn
Car son a bhiodh sinn bronach?
Ach siùd agaibh an t-achmhasan
Thug brathair m'athar dhiomhsa

'Dheanadh i dhuit deasachadh
Is loisg' i beagan moine
Is bhiodh an dinnear deas aice
'S feitheamh ort an comhnuidh?'
'Cha n'eisd mi ri do leisgeulan
Tha taigh agad an ordugh
'S ged bhristeadh i na soitheachean

Learning the Language

Tha'n choire sin aig moran
'Bruidhinn socair reidh rithe
'S mas fheudar e, bheir pog dhi,
Is coma leat bhith beulach
Ri gach uile té as boidhche'

O! ni sinn faighidinn,
Car son a bhiodh sinn brònach
Ach siud agaibh an t-achmhasan
Thug mac brathair m'athar dhomhsa

The Rebuke

Thus spoke cousin Alasdair,
He said that I was foolish,
Prodigiously stupid,
Staying on my lonesome
'If you had a wife now
Who would stay beside you
You'd not be cold or hungry
From Saturday to Sunday'
Oh well, let's be patient
Why should we be gloomy?
But that is the rebuke that
My cousin went and gave me

'But if she does the needful
And few peats she is burning
Gets dinner ready for you
And is always waiting on you?
I'm tired of your excuses,
Your house is in good order
And if she breaks the dishes,
Well, that's the fault of many'
Speak nice and gently to her,
And kiss her if you need to

And flatter her regardless –
It's loved by every woman'

Ach well, let's be patient
Why should we be gloomy?
But that is the reproach that
My cousin went and gave me

Not every local versifier was as accomplished as the Bard, but that did not mean that their more occasional output was not just as appreciated for its humour, including the odd poem in English such as that which Alasdair Buie, an uncle of Big Peter, composed about life in Glassard very shortly after the Riasg Buidhe folk had moved over to live there, and which was recited to me by *Morag Cholla,* Morag daughter of Old Coll MacAllister, the evening I recorded her.

Oh, I long to be in Glassard where the noisy blackbird
   sings,
Where the cattle eat their breakfast and the seagulls flap
   their wings,
Where Jimmy Reid's a-sitting in another person's house
A-waiting for his dinner as quiet as a mouse,
Where Para Mor's a-praying for his cannibalistic soul
And though he isn't working he never draws the dole,
Where Coll's children are a-playing around the rolling sea
And the Bard is making poetry and drinking lots of tea,
Where Aldy is a-playing upon his 'Melodyman'
And the 'Sassenach' is beating upon a frying pan.

(The Para Mor referred to here was Big Peter's uncle and the 'Sassenach' his father, John – a nickname given to him by the 'Sassenach's' wife, Ina, before they were married, as a comment on how much time he had to spend way from the island working on the mainland. The 'Melodyman' was a melodeon, a type of accordion.)

Though home-grown versification was still prized and remembered by the older islanders, it may have been a symptom of the decline in the population of Gaelic speakers and tradition-bearers that there were so few practitioners left on the island apart from Donald 'Garvard'. However, old Ross Darroch, who would successfully turn his hand to anything, did still occasionally produce a topical verse or two in Gaelic, English or a free and easy mix of the two, and he brought the pub to a pint-spluttering standstill one February evening when he announced to the assembly that he had composed a chorus but needed help with the verses.

The subject of the poem was one which Ross knew was close to my heart, as I had quite unexpectedly found myself cast as central figure in an outlandishly scripted episode of the island's drama one unusually hard and frosty winter of relentless east wind – the island was, unbelievably, under attack from otters! At least the island's chickens and ducks were, as the otters which were commonly seen around the shores of the island, including the harbour when it was quiet, were evidently finding fish in short supply and had started raiding several island henhouses in different parts of the island. We ourselves had lost almost all of our beloved birds one night when an otter stove in a weak plank at the bottom of our henhouse and, pausing only to despatch all but two of the rest of our hens, had carried one away with him – oblivious that he had left his paw-prints in the fresh snow plus a telltale trail of feathers leading past the pottery and round the harbour shore. He was guilty as charged, and I was determined to stop him doing it again.

On advice from Ross, the master rabbit trapper, I made a snare out of a length of old clutch cable and set it in a freshwater run in the rocks near the harbour which I knew the otter used. I was more than a little startled to discover next morning that it had worked, and I then had to steel myself to finish the large dog otter off cleanly with my shotgun. Ross appeared genuinely impressed with the big-game hunter outcome and I knew it would make the lead story in the *Colonsay Gazette* that day, but there was more to come. The following morning I got a call from farmer Alastair McNeill (known locally as 'Alastair

Machrins') to tell me that 'you'd better come quick, Potter, and bring your gun', as they had just discovered that another cheeky otter which had been helping itself to the farm's hens was still sleeping off its full stomach in some hay in the selfsame farm's steading – a piece of temerity if ever there was one. An emergency farmhouse conference had concluded that if they poked it awake with a pitchfork and then chased it through the steading door then someone with a shotgun – who better than the island's self-appointed otter-slayer – could finish it off; which is what transpired after I had driven full throttle down the long straight to Machrins Farm.

Ross seemed even more impressed and was sufficiently moved, if not to verse, then to a chorus which he decided, without any forewarning, to premier before a full but unsuspecting audience in the pub the following Saturday evening and it went to the tune of 'She'll be coming round the mountain when she comes'. As ever, Ross's utterance was delivered with word, syllable, consonant and vowel-perfect clarity, with extra lip-smacking relish and resonance being applied to the key words, otter, potter and ball – 'ball' being pronounced like the French pronunciation of Basle, the city in Switzerland, but with a breathy aspiration preceding the lengthened 'aa' sound. It went like this and I hear him yet:

> 'Ach, the otter's got the potter by the bhaaalls,
> Ach, the otter's got the potter by the bhaaalls
> Though the potter shot the otter
> Well, the otter's got the potter
> And the otter's got the potter by the bhaaaaaaalls!'

Ross's inimitable rendition and climax, complete with appropriately placed hand movements, would have done Pavarotti proud and, no less the maestro, brought the house down – and with it any sense of conceit which a puffed-up otter-slayer might just have been inclined to assume.

4

WHAT'S IN A NAME?

As I listened, every day that passed, to the rich conversational flow of the older islanders, the narrative they wove around island life teemed with references not just to other islanders – both the living and those still alive in their long memories – but to countless island places as well, each one with its own unique name and precise location. The placenames they used seemed to have a life of their own and told stories within stories. In any event, they cast their spell on me and made me want to get to know them better.

Remarkably, it seemed like it might be a fairly straightforward task because 'Loder', the name by which John de Vere Loder's great book *Colonsay and Oronsay* is commonly referred to by the locals who use it, contains a list of over 1,650 placenames with their English translations. The names had been gathered by Murdo McNeill, *Murchadh Chalum* as he was always called by the native Gaels, who had painstakingly inscribed them all onto a 6-inch map kept in Colonsay Estate Office. I soon discovered, however, that this priceless piece of Colonsay's heritage had been burnt with the rubbish following an over-enthusiastic spring clean, instigated, it was alleged, by a former Estate Factor. So, with all the initial fervour of a new convert I decided to have a go at re-collecting both the names and, critically, the locations of as many of those places which still formed a natural part of the shared consciousness of the last generations of islanders whose mother tongue was Colonsay Gaelic.

That placenames were even more abundant and well-used just a few generations before was pointed out by Murchadh

Chalum who wrote in his book 'it has been asserted that the places in Balnahard (*Baile na h-airde*, "peninsula township" which is the northernmost section of Colonsay) had formerly been so well-named in detail that the people without difficulty could apportion the land as they sat on *Cnoc a chreagain*, "hill of the little rock", "Yea, even to the breadth of a *caibe* (spade) handle".' This must have been in the early nineteenth century before the time that what subsequently became Balnahard Farm was cleared by the McNeill lairds of its numerous runrig-crofting tenants. 28 families had left Balnahard on the one day, so I was told by *Niall a Ghoirtean* (Neil Martin of the croft called 'goirtean' – one of many Gaelic words for a field), who was born in the early 1890s and had been told the story by his grandfather, a witness to the event.

In the 1970s most of the older islanders still knew and drew effortlessly on their lifetime accumulations of different place-names, in particular of those island areas in which they had either lived or worked in or both, and therefore knew intimately. The longer a corner of the island had been occupied by an indigenous family, the greater the likelihood that its names and their locations and some of the stories that went with them would be remembered. Thus, for example, in Colonsay's two remaining continuously crofted areas, Kilchattan and Uragaig, older crofters like Neil Martin, Dougie McGilvray, Donald 'Gibby' McNeill, Dolly Ann MacDougall and her daughter, Ina Williams, could recall the names and, thankfully, the locations of several hundred places: fields, fanks, shielings, marshes, streams, fords, lochs, pools, wells, hills, Iron-Age forts and fortlets, Celtic churches, fairy knolls, hill passes, gates, terraces, cliffs, paths, ridges, caves, ruins, old kelp-burning kilns, standing stones, cairns, cliffs, rocks, skerries, islets, bays, beaches, channels, creeks, tide markers, natural harbours, landing places, fishing rocks, sunken reefs and lobster holes and more besides, each topographical feature carrying its homegrown and distinguishing appellation.

So too did the fishermen, like the two Peters MacAllister – *Para Mor*/'Big Peter' or his uncle, 'Old Peter' MacAllister – carry and still use a shared lexicon of placenames for their extensive fishing areas and stretches of coastline; not just each and every waiting rock and skerry but even permanently submerged points of reference, like the *rocs*, the 'sunken reefs', that made good fishing spots, or the *faicheachean,* the special holes in the rocks from which a lobster might be extricated with a *cliob*, a home-made lobster hook, at low water during spring tides. In fact the word *faiche* means a 'burrow' because, within living memory, so I was assured, lobsters had once been so numerous that they used to make burrows in the sand to take their cover.

The placenames quest I set out on fed my imagination every bit as much as my desire to be able to incorporate these hidden signposts, which dotted the island landscape and seascape, into my own inner satnav. *Meall na suiridhe,* the 'headland of the wooing' in Balnahard and *Bruach a' ghaoil,* 'the hillside of love' in Oronsay were both green and pastoral slopes where the mind's eye could easily picture the young lovers who went courting there in those early nineteenth century times when Colonsay and Oronsay supported a permanent population nearly ten times the size of the number left living there in the 1970s. There was even *clach an tairbh,* 'the bull's stone', a smooth boulder by the side of the road that runs down to the tidal strand that joins Colonsay to Oronsay. This was where a so-nicknamed Lothario of yesteryear was wont to take a breather on his perambula-tions, so my informant old Ross Darroch assured me, because his great-grandmother, *Floraidh Bhuie* or 'Flora Buie' – who had been born nearby in a place called the *buth beag,* 'the wee shop', long since abandoned and with hardly a trace left in the land-scape but still with its historically interesting name and location intact – had told him.

I soon became hooked by these journeys of discovery which the placenames proffered. They preserved much interesting information, and even though there the was the frustration of realising that the locations or the community's recollection of some of Murchadh Chalum's lovingly gathered names had been lost it was satisfying to be able to put a place back together with its name or even, every now and then, find a totally new one with an explanatory story attached – such as the one which Ross Darroch told me as a coda to his reminiscence about *clach an tairbh*. This was about another roadside resting place, *Creag Eoghann Ghoraidh*, 'Hugh son of Godfrey's rock', which is an outcrop that still fringes the single track road not far from Machrins Farmhouse and was where Eoghann, a nineteeth century packman, would habitually stop to lay down the pack he carried on his back and have what old Aldy MacAllister – who had a great memory for placenames – used to call a *suidheachean*, 'a wee sit down and a breather', and which he used to take himself on his walks to collect his pension from the post office then in Glassard.

Hugh's pack would be full of goods from the mainland to sell to interested islanders, and even as late as the 1970s, Colonsay was still visited by packmen in all but name. The last in the line was Abdul Karim, who every six months or so would emerge from the ferry wheeling his old black bicycle weighed down, though still just about rideable, with two shiny, brown leather suitcases stuffed full of clothing options for all ages strapped on the back of the bike. Rain, shine or gale, he would push it up the hills, ride it on a flat bit and patiently make his way right round the island to every single inhabited house, where he was welcomed back as an old friend and encouraged to open up his suitcases for the close inspection and inevitable purchases which followed. Eoghann Ghoraidh would have been proud of him and surely received the same warm island welcome in his day.

The landscape was full of unwritten but still tangible records revealing aspects of the once real and vivid lives of previous generations of islanders, whose self-reliance and hard graft are commemorated in names like *Lochan an lion,* 'the little lint loch' just north of Garvard Farmhouse. Here flax plants were once steeped as part of the exhaustive process undertaken in turning the flax plant into linen such as the communion tablecloth, the last known locally produced piece, that is still used in Colonsay's Church of Scotland.

In an unattributed (but it surely has to be written by Professor MacKinnon) March 1911 *Glasgow Herald* article, which formed part of a small treasure chest of similar cuttings and memorabilia collected over the years by Big Peter's family and preserved in an old-fashioned biscuit tin kept ever-handy for occasional reference, the Professor recollects that 'of all the duties that fell to the housewife's lot, none taxed her time and strength in a greater degree while it lasted than the preparation of lint, the indispensable flax plant. In this district [one of Peter's forebears had pencilled in 'Colonsay'] its cultivation ceased about 60 years ago. When the flax was ripe it was hand-pulled and tied up in small sheaves until such time as was found convenient to commence "rippling", the process by which the seed capsules were stripped off the stalks. "Retting" followed; the bundles of the flax were immersed in pools of standing water in an adjacent peat bog and allowed to soak for a couple of weeks until the woody portion of the stem had decomposed sufficiently. It was then spread out on the ground to dry. Drying was sometimes hastened by artificial means in primitive grain-drying kilns in use at that period, the flax spread out on improvised rafters and a fire lighted underneath, care being exercised to prevent the whole thing taking fire – a calamity not unheard of.' When the flax was dry and crisp enough it was ready for 'breaking' by bashing it with a wooden lump hammer on a hard surface. The next part of the process, 'scutching', involved using a two-foot long wooden scutching sword and scutching block to remove as much of the woody portion from the fibre as possible, after which it was drawn several times through another 'stripping' tool. Now it was ready for 'heckling', requiring the application of two sorts of heckles or metal combs, one with strong teeth like nails, the other fine.

Eventually it was ready for spinning and the Professor observed 'when a person had much of this kind of work to do, a time was set for doing it, assistance being readily given by neighbours, who, bringing their spinning wheels along with them to the house where the work was being done, worked blithely together, often the entire night, until the quality of thread desired for the weaver was spun. Such gatherings, which were characteristic of the times, were social events as well; songs composed for the occasion were sung, old tales recited and it may be taken for granted where so many of the gentler sex forgathered, references to the latest and most interesting events of the hour intermittently made.' The article concludes 'from fibre well dressed, linen of good quality is said to have been produced. The finest in texture was made into shirts and other articles of personal wear and domestic use and the strongest into sheets. For bleaching it was boiled with kelp from the knobbed seaweed. Needless to say the work connected with the preparation of lint and wool demanded close application, deftness of fingers and practical skill in no small degree. It was the housewife's ambition to turn out every member of the family in a new outfit of homespun on New Year's Day – then kept on January 12th or 13th – and where the family was large this was no small undertaking.'

Luba na seicheachan, 'pool of the hides', is a brackish rock-pool, though well above high water mark, which lies a little way west of Ardskenish Farmhouse and is the place where cattle hides were steeped as part of the leather-making process that kept the island cobblers supplied. The last in the line was the father of *Sandy Greusaich,* 'Sandy the Cobbler's son', who lived and worked in Scalasaig's Squint Street in the latter half of the nineteenth century.

There are several shoreline remnants too of the kelp industry that flourished in the Hebrides in the early 1800s, and of the shallow, stone-lined pits or 'kilns', a couple of metres or so in length, and though long since grown over still identifiable, where dried-out seaweed previously gathered in from the shore was burnt to produce a residue which was sold for soap production. *An athach cealp,* 'the kelp kiln' is still clearly discernible on the eastern side of Oronsay adjacent to *Port na h-ath,* 'kiln harbour' and Seal Cottage, as is another *athach cealp* on the Garvard shore of the Strand, this time with a stone-built rock shelter not far away known as *tigh na cealpairean,* 'the kelp-makers house';

though it is but a poor relation of the ruin of the same name which still stands on *Eilean nan Ron*, 'Seal Island' which lies to the south of Oronsay.

An t-seann ceardaich, 'the old smithy', lies on the south side of the Scalasaig lighthouse point and pinpoints the place where the quarrying and associated masonry work was carried out in the mid-nineteenth century to shape the blocks for the 'new' harbour and breakwater constructed around *Port na feamuinn* in Scalasaig – where I watched all the comings and goings through the open door of my boathouse turned pottery. *Gart a ghobhainn,* 'the blacksmith's patch' overlooking *Port Mor,* 'big (natural) harbour' on Colonsay's west side, would have been very familiar to the boys who went to the long-since obliterated school next door, one of whom in the 1840s was the young Donald McKinnon, the crofter's son who went on to become the professor.

Bruthach an t-seanna mhuilinn, 'Brae of the old mill', located where the track through Colonsay Gardens drops down to cross the burn, recalls the medieval mill which must once have served the monks of Kiloran Abbey, which formerly occupied the site of Colonsay House, the gradually extended mansion house which was once home to the McNeills and to this day their successor lairds, the Strathconas. Further up the burn the McNeill lairds built a new mill, since resurrected from the ruin it became and converted into a pretty house; and the same burn that fed both mills assumes five different names on its barely two-mile journey from its source at *Loch a Sgoltaire,* 'Loch of the Cleaver', to its escape into the sea at the southern corner of Kiloran Bay. As it runs from its starting point down through the long-since cleared crofting township of *A' Bheinn a Tuath,* 'The North peak', the burn is called *Abhainn nan doidean,* 'burn of the small crofts'; when it reaches the road and the converted mill it becomes *Abhainn a mhuilinn,* 'the mill stream'; where it passes under the road by the old village hall at Kiloran it becomes *Abhainn a bhroghain,* derivation unclear; as it wends its way through Colonsay Gardens and past the site of the old mill it becomes *Abhainn a mhuilinn* again, although the mill referred to is now the medieval one; and, finally, as it nears the road junction with the track that leads up to Balnahard, it becomes *Abhainn a chroiseain,* 'the burn of the cross'. The name commemorates a long-vanished cross that must have stood in the adjacent field, known to this day as *pairc a chroisean,* 'field of the little cross', and which perhaps once marked a geographical limit of the authority of the long-vanished abbey.

We can be sure that many of the local placenames are many hundreds of years old, some a thousand years and more. The Irish saints of the early Celtic Church gave their names to a host of churches in the Highlands and Islands and beyond. The first churches were built in wattle, then replaced by stone-built ones; their tell-tale 'Kil' prefixes deriving from the old Gaelic word *cille,* which originally denoted a small 'cell' of monks or nuns who first raised their church in the name of one or other revered saint. Within the narrow confines of Colonsay and Oronsay, more than a dozen early Celtic churches have left their place-names, though not always their visible remains, behind. Saint Oran gave his name to Kiloran, *Cill Odhrain,* and its aforementioned Abbey. Not far from Balnahard Farmhouse, the Colonsay home of Professor McKinnon, lie the ruins of *Cill' Chatriona*, a church dedicated by its attendant cell of nuns to Saint Catherine. Saints Kenneth, Kiaran, Bridget and Maelruba gave their names to churches, respectively *Cille Choinnich, Cille Chiarain, Cille Bhride* and *Cille Rubha*, of which few traces now remain, though their locations more or less do. Oronsay or *Orasaigh,* however, with its famous priory, did not get its name from Saint Oran but from the Norse *Orfiris-ey* which signifies an island – of which there are several examples in the Northern and Western Isles – which can be walked over to once the tide has gone out, as over 'the Strand': *An fhaoghail,* the beautiful expanse of sand that joins Colonsay to Oronsay and its once famous Priory.

Here it may be noted that the islanders themselves often had more than one name to distinguish themselves from other island-ers and for general third party reference. There were, for example, four different Colonsay Donald McNeills to be distinguished:

Donald 'Gibby', Donald 'Garvard', Donald Garvard's son 'Peedie', and Donald 'Gartcosh', who had lived for many years in Gartcosh near Glasgow. Donald 'Gibby' was the son of Gilbert or Gibby McNeill, and Donald Garvard was so named after his farm, and although older islanders still called him Donald Oronsay after the island of his upbringing, the same much-loved Donald was also universally referred to as 'D.A.', his initials, giving him the grand, but for the uninitiated somewhat confusing, total of four different working appellations. Between nicknames, additions to first names like old, young, big and wee, or by nouns denoting to which family the person belonged, you could be excused for thinking that the resident population was at least twice the size it really was. The new family in Glen Cottage soon got the hang of it, however, and in their turn were accorded their own local soubriquets derived from the trade of the householder, whose spouse was accordingly referred to in the third person as *bean a photter,* 'the potter's wife', with a similar application to our three children as they arrived to take their places in the community: Danny Photter, Katie Photter and Georgie Photter.

To be added to the cast of living islanders were a host of antecedents, some going back generations, whose names also provided links to a way of life that was a still-remembered part of the island's heritage. The Miller, the Shoemaker, the Blacksmith, the Schoolmaster, the Butler, the Gardener, the Captain, the Mate, the Bard, the Carpenter and the Professor and their family members were all recalled by names which evoked a fairly recent and much busier and more self-sufficient island world. Nicknames abounded too, like the Blonkan, Boig, Doshie and Punch, and the *Cra-gheadh,* 'the shelduck', who was a favourite island schoolmistress in the 1930s. Sometimes the names went in pairs like the 'the Black 'un and the White 'un', the two McLaughlan sisters who had farmed Ardskenish; or 'the F and Ms', as the two McNeill sisters who had run the hotel in the early years of the twentieth century were always referred to.

In the long and scholarly series of articles written by the Professor on 'Place Names and Personal Names in Argyll' and published by *The Scotsman* in 1887, he forensically unravels the meaning of many local placenames, like *Crois an Tearmaid,* 'the Sanctuary Cross' which lies halfway across the Strand. He writes, 'The land granted to the founder of a church as an endowment was called the *termon* land, from the Latin, *terminus,* "a limit". As we find from the Gaelic entries in the Book of Deer, such lands were free from rents, exactions or tributes. These lands also carried the right of sanctuary and hence the meaning of *tearmunn* in modern Gaelic of "refuge" and "protection", the original signification of "sanctuary".'

He tells us too that 'In addition to *Cille,* a derivative form *cealltrach* is used in Ireland to denote an old burying ground. The form is hardly used in Scotland though there is a *Lochan na cealltrach* in Oronsay, a pool which lies near the faintest outline of *Cille Mhoire*, "St Mary's Church" and not that far from *Port Mhorein*, the "harbour of St Mary's follower".' There is another slightly more discernible *Cille Mhoire* in front of Kilchattan Primary School, although the ruined *Cille Chattan*, 'Church dedicated to Saint Catan' lies in the corner of the 'old' graveyard which overlooks *Port Mor*.

The wishing well, *Tobar Chaluim Chille*, 'Saint Columba's Well', is located a little way north of Kiloran Bay. It is just one of forty wells whose unique names were gathered by Murchadh Chalum and which are preserved for posterity in Loder's book, although the precise locations of many of them have now been lost. Columba is also remembered as having first stopped in Colonsay on his self-imposed journey of exile from Ireland, making landfall in a place called *Port na h-Iubhraich*, 'Barge harbour', on the north side of the south-western tip of the island. He is then said to have crossed over the Strand to Oronsay where he founded a monastery on the site of the later Augustinian priory, but when he discovered on climbing Oronsay's highest hill that he could still see the tops of the Blue Mountains of his beloved Donegal poking up behind the intervening Isle of Islay, he decided, with some reluctance, surely, to set sail again for Iona, where he finally settled and founded his world-famous monastery. The cairn on top of the hill he climbed is known to this day as *Carn cul ri Eirinn*, cairn with its back to Ireland.

Oronsay itself has a wealth of gathered and recorded place-names, thanks not only to the painstaking efforts of Murchadh Chalum but to the family of McNeills who farmed the island for several generations. When I set out upon my own quest during the 1970s, I was greatly helped and encouraged by 'Donald Garvard' McNeill who then farmed Garvard, but was a born and bred native of Oronsay and scion of its farming family, like his sister, Flora, who still lived and farmed on Oronsay with her husband Andrew till they retired at end of the seventies and moved to Glassard. *Glais-aird* is translated in Loder as 'grey cape', but might equally well be translated as 'green quarter', the word *glais* being used to describe the duller versions of green as well as rock-grey, both of which can be found in Glassard. Donald not only happily shared the names and locations of Oronsay's places plus many more from the southern reaches of Colonsay, but he tape-recorded them all – plus the many more gathered for Colonsay – reading more than a thousand of them out in the clearest and purest Colonsay/Oronsay Gaelic, and finishing off with a humorous Gaelic song, replete with placename references, that features *Sandy Greusaich,* 'Sandy, the shoemaker's son'. The tape was duly deposited with the School of Scottish Studies along with the large-scale maps capturing all the names and locations gathered. What pleasure I had, taking advantage of the extra opportunities the quest gave me to blether and enjoy the company and insights of dozens of Colonsay's and Oronsay's native and expatriate Gaels, without whose help and kindness it would not have been possible and infinitely less enjoyable, and whose names are also faithfully recorded. Looking back, I only wish that I had been wider awake and noted down the stories that flowed from many of their placename references and to which I am unable to do justice.

For anyone who may be as intrigued as I was and wish to study them or other placenames in other parts, I would only offer encouragement, because it is a rich seam that brings its own special rewards. My particular favourites are the ones that excite the imagination, get you puzzling and have more than one meaning to give the more you think about them. *Glaic an taghain*, 'the marten's dell' in Scalasaig, *Lag nam feocullan*, 'the polecats' hollow' in Oronsay, tell of creatures that became extinct within the historical period of human occupation of these islands; whereas *Sguid pioghaid*, 'magpie shelter' in Kiloran refers to a change in the island's birdlife, which might however be reversed at some point. In his article on 'Archaic Words and Forms', the Professor also refers to the crane, a long-vanished bird which once must have been common enough, at least during the period of the islands' Norse occupancy. It gave its name to *Eilean Tranaig*, 'crane bay island' from the Norse *trana-vik*, which lies in the mouth of *Port na blathach*, 'buttermilk harbour' at Oronsay's south-west corner.

The Professor goes on to say 'In Colonsay there is a *torr an tuirc*, "the boar's heap", and at a quarter of a mile's distance *torr na baine*, "baine" being the genitive of *banbh*, "a young pig", a word utterly unknown in Scottish Gaelic.' Almost as an aside, he then adds, '*Coll*, Welsh *coll*, English *hazel*, is a living word in Irish but obsolete with us. In Colonsay, *Glaic a' chuill*, "hazel hollow", appears twice and one is tempted to ask whether the name of the island is not derived from this root.' Although the Professor goes on to say that 'Colonsay might also be *Colin's isle*', his friend and another Professor, William J. Watson, Scotland's renowned toponymist and author of *The History of Celtic Place-names*, advised Loder that he was 'certain that Colonsay means Kolbein's Isle. Kolbein is Norse and is the original of the modern name Colvin.' The intrusive 'n' in some but not all of the earliest recorded versions of the name 'Colonsay' would seem to tip the balance firmly towards Professor Watson's explanation, but part of the fun of collecting and musing upon placenames is being able to make one's own speculations, no matter how unprofessorial, and it may be worth pondering that if a superfluous 'n' somehow found its way into the documented transcription of *Orasa* or *Orasaigh*, the Gael's spoken version of Oronsay, then the same might have happened with *Colosa* or *Colosaigh*, the Gael's version of Colonsay. It has also been suggested that *Colla*, whose Iron Age fort, *Dun Cholla,* stands proud to this day overlooking the Strand, may also have given his name to Colonsay. He may very well not have, but is his claim any weaker than Kolbein's? Who was this Kolbein, that he was important enough to give his name to the island but left no other tradition or placename behind him? And then there's Earl Gilli of the Icelandic sagas, an important Norse chieftain who may well have made Colonsay his home and southern power-base but also left no local tradition or placename clue. And what about the place called *Colosus* by Saint Adomnan in his *Life of Saint Columba* which he wrote in the seventh century? Here enthusiastic amateur speculation takes a rest, but you get the idea.

What is certain is that the Norsemen settled and intermixed with the Gaelic-speaking population the length and breadth of the Hebrides and far beyond. It is perhaps unsurprising that even though their Norse language must have been spoken in the islands for centuries, alongside if not entirely instead of the surviving Gaelic language, comparatively few Norse placenames have survived to the present day. Balnahard has a notably large share of them and perhaps this suggests that it was the final redoubt of Colonsay's last remaining Norse-speakers. During the summer months, so old Peter MacAllister told me, the Professor used to moor his skiff at the north end of Balnahard Bay in *Poll na cnarradh*, 'Pool of the vessel', *knarr* being the Norse word for 'vessel', which shows that this anchorage sheltered by *sgeir Nic Fhionnlaidh*, 'Finlay's daughter's skerry' had been used by Gaels and Norsemen for hundreds of years. Just a little further up the coast, *Caisebrig* and *Croisebrig* lie next to each other: *Caisebrig* meaning 'Stone-heap slope' from the Norse '*kasa-brekka*', and *Croisebrig* meaning 'Cross slope' from the Norse '*crossa-brekka*'.

With the licence to speculate and digress that is the privilege of all amateur placename enthusiasts, I wonder whether the fact that there was once a landmark cross on this slope and that it was probably *in situ* long before the first Norsemen had logged it as they sailed by, named it and had driven their longships onto the clean, white sand of Balnahard Bay in order to have a closer look and, more importantly, to explore the entrepreneurial opportunities waiting for them a bit further inland, means that it was already there for a reason? And the reason must surely have been that it marked the presence down in the rocky shoreline below of the well-hidden *Uamh Chorpach*, 'The cave of the corpses', complete to this day with the stone slabs upon which the bodies of monks and/or nuns were laid before they were taken on to Iona for burial, when the sea and wind conditions in the open Atlantic beyond the north tip of Colonsay permitted. In any event, the *croisebrig* cross must have been a sufficiently useful landmark to save it from being knocked down in a fit of pagan pique by magic mushroom-fuelled Vikings, even though there is no trace of it left today except, thankfully, its thought-provoking name.

And how about the derivation of Uragaig overlooking Kiloran Bay? The 'aig' ending is the Norse for bay, but the 'Ura' prefix offers no certain Norse clues, and could it be that it is a surviving remnant of the language that was spoken before the Gaelic-speakers arrived? Does it have the same root as *uamh* (very roughly pronounced 'oo-ah'), the onomatopoeic Gaelic word for cave; for the two headlands embracing Kiloran Bay contain a dozen caves between them, each with their uniquely descriptive Gaelic names such as *an uamh na mine, an uamh shiorruidh* and *an uamh cramhaich*; respectively 'the cave of the bag(s) of meal', 'the endless cave' and 'the chough cave'? Many of the caves reveal evidence of human habitation going back to the very first people to set foot and live on the islands after the last Ice Age, perhaps even pre-dating the pioneers who left behind the huge shell middens on Oronsay which the later Gaels called *Sithean*, 'fairy knoll', by way of non-archaeological explanation. The longest cave is called the *Uamh Ur*, which can be readily translated from Gaelic as the 'new cave', which makes little sense unless the 'ur' bit of the name pre-dates the Gaelic language and its real meaning is 'cave cave'. Such musings soon become second nature to the placename prospector, and it is all too easy to get carried away.

Not far short of the northernmost point of Balnahard there is a green isthmus called *Iamalum*, 'lamb's holm' – a holm being a Norse word with two meanings: a piece of flat ground that is subject to flooding, and a small round island. This particular isthmus is not infrequently lashed and washed over from west to east by wild winter seas, but further down Colonsay's east coast lies *Eilean Olmsa*, a Gaelic-Norse mix meaning 'island [Gaelic] of the small round island [Norse]' and shows how Norse placenames were remembered by Colonsay Gaels who no longer understood Norse. Even the pronunciation of some of these preserved placenames is still authentically Norse, suggesting that they may have become cemented by familiar usage during a long period of Gaelic-Norse bilingualism and fluency. The Professor tells us that 'Among the many words borrowed by Highlanders from the Norse is *Gja*, "a chasm", now applied to a steep narrow creek or gully. The present Gaelic form is *geodha, a* changed to *o*. The old sound is, however, preserved in a place-name in Colonsay – *Rudha Gheadha*, "the point of the *gja*", the headland, complete with said gully, which guards the southern approach to Balnahard Bay.'

Norse personal names are preserved too in *Scalasaig*, 'Skalli's [meaning 'Baldyhead's] Bay' and *Dun Eibhinn,* Scalasaig's impressive Iron Age fort, which Professor Watson says means 'Eyvind's Fort', and speaks of a period in Colonsay's history when the Norse hegemony was at its most powerful and Eyvind was the island's big cheese. The two islands are almost as full of *Duns* (pronounced 'doons') as there are Celtic churches, and the Professor refers to one of the equally numerous *Dunans*, 'little fortlets', which were connected to one or other of the main forts but are less well known, including *Dunan na Fidean*, next door to the place where people park their cars prior to walking across the Strand. 'In Icelandic,' the Professor explains, '*fit* means the web on the feet of web-footed birds and, metaphorically, meadow land on the banks of a firth or lake which are occasionally subject to flooding. In the sheltered, shallow windings of the Western Isles, the tide at high spring insinuates itself along narrow creeks far into the land, leaving here and there green tongues and islets uncovered. Such plots are called by the Gaelic people *fidean,* the "webs" so to speak of the claws of the sea,' a good description of this particular corner of the Strand.

Other once real live Colonsay people are also recalled by places associated with them. For example, *Rubha Dheorsa,* 'George's point' and *Roc Dheorsa,* 'George's sunken reef' lie below Glassard and are named, so the late Mary Clark told me, after her maternal great-grandfather, George Buchanan, who lived in Glassard in the nineteenth century. *Carnan 'Harty',* with the personal name invariably pronounced 'hair-ty' with the characteristic flattening of the vowel that Colonsay Gaelic gives to many of its 'a' sounds, is a small cairn constructed on the rocky shore below Baleromindubh, *Baile Raomuinn Dubh,* 'Black Raymond's homestead/township'; and not to be confused with the name of the neighbouring farm, *Baile Raomuinn Mor,* 'Big Raymond's homestead/township'. Nothing more is remembered about either Raymond who, sixteenth-century deed records of Colonsay farm names and rentals show, must have lived at least five hundred years ago, but Captain Harty was involved in the oceanographic survey which produced the first Admiralty chart of the local waters in 1855 and built the eponymous cairn. It is fitting, perhaps, that in the traditional homeland of the MacPhee clan, no single personal name occurs more frequently, albeit for sad reasons. Malcolm, the last of the Colonsay MacPhee chieftains was hunted and murdered by a gang led by *Colla Ciotach,* 'left-handed Coll' MacDonald in February 1623. In his protracted bid to escape his pursuers the MacPhee used a series of hiding places – six in Colonsay, one in Oronsay – which are recorded to this day in the same placename, *Leab' fhalaich Mhic a Phie,* literally 'MacPhee's hiding bed' because he would use them to lie low there day and night.

Every single name adds to sense and understanding of place – some more prosaically than others, it has to be admitted, but that may only be because one isn't subjecting them to close enough examination. At their best, placenames work themselves into your imagination and bring an extra dimension to the way that you see and enjoy the landscape. *Druim buiteachean,* 'the witches' ridge' to the right on the way to Kiloran Bay, never fails to deliver a frisson, if only because *Glaic nan cnamh,* 'the dell of bones' and *Cnoc seunta,* 'the enchanted hill' lie not much further on. Though I reserve the right to disbelieve that fairy creatures known as the *Glaiserig,* 'Grey slinking one' and the *'gruagach',* 'long-haired one' ever existed, I am still enchanted to know that the former lived just behind *Gart a gobhainn* in *Slochd na Glaiserig*, 'the Glaisrig's gulley', and the latter had a special boulder called *Clach na Gruagach*, 'the Gruagach's stone', where every evening a libation of fresh milk was poured for her into a basin-like hole in case she made life difficult for both cattle and people.

There is poetry too in placenames: *Gob a chlachairain*, 'the bill of the little mason' (the Gaelic name given to the wheatear), which knocks spots off 'Avenue Cottage', the name by which this cottage is now called; or *sruthan a bhalbhain*, 'the deaf mute's streamlet', which flows under the road between the shop and Glassard; or *Lagan soilleir doilleir*, 'light and shade little hollow', that lies below and beyond Oronsay Farm and not that far from *Tobair na biolaire*, 'watercress well'. However, anyone still doubting the magical power of Colonsay and Oronsay's placenames might wish to ponder the thought that an invocation of placenames was once, tradition has it, successfully deployed to repel an invasion by raiders from the island of Mull, a not infrequent occurrence, it seems, in days gone by. I was given this story by the late Duncan 'Dotie' McNeill, brother of Donald 'Gibby' McNeill, whose father Gilbert or 'Gibby' had written it down in Gaelic and it goes like this.

Bha uair Muileaich a tighinn do Colosa; Bha bean airigh air mullach Cailleach Uragaig is i gamharc oire gu iosal agus thoisich i air deanadh agus aig a cheart am air gabhail ranntachd mar seo,

Agus thoisich i air deanadh agus aig a cheart am air gabhail ranntachd mar seo:

> *Druim buiteachean is Lag nan Goirteanean,*
> *(Fonn) Am ba on Raoil Oig,*
> *Na tri faing ri taobh an locha,*
> *Cnoc Thalanta★ mhor 'san deanadh an crochadh,*
> *(Fonn) Am ba on Raoil Oig,*
> *Mullaraich is Tullaraich,*
> *(Fonn) Am ba on Raoil Oig,*
> *A Bheinn Bhreac is Torr an Tuirc*
> *Far am bi na h'uile a gabhail tamh,*
> *Giraig is Goraig is Grianaig,★*
> *Taobh an iar Phort na Fliuchan*
> *(Fonn) Am ba on Raoil Oig.*

Ghabh na Muileaich an t-eagal gu an robh uidhmeachddh nach cordadh riu a deanadh rompa agus rinn iad a reir an t-seann fhacal 'Tilleadh math seadh droch fhuireachd' agus thill iad dhachaidh gun feuchainn ri tighinn air tir idir

The Mull men were coming to Colonsay one time, there was a sheiling-lady on top of [a face-like headland called] 'the old woman of Uragaig' and she was looking down below (at where the Mull men's boats were coming into land) and she started to compose and at the same time start chanting this verse:

★Almost all the placenames and locations in this several hundred years-old story are still remembered except for '*Lag nan Goirtenean*' and '*Giraig*'. The 'three fank fields' are in Kiloran and are known individually as the West Fank, East Fank and Big Fank, *Faing an iar, Faing an ear* and *Faing Mor. Cnoc Thalanta* or *Cnoc Callanta* as it is written on modern OS maps and is remembered as a hangman's hill, though the derivation of the name is not clear.

Witches' ridge and fields of the hollow,
(Chorus) The lullaby of Young Ranald,
The three fank-fields beside the loch,
? Hill, where they do the hanging,
Hill-top sheiling and north-facing shieling,
The Speckled Peak and the Boar's Mound
Where everyone can find peace,
? And 'Sunny harbour'
On the west side of 'Wetness harbour'
(Chorus) The lullaby of Young Ranald

The Mull men took fright that preparations were being made which wouldn't agree with them and they took heed of the old saying 'When staying where you are is a bad idea then it's a good idea to go home', and so they returned whence they came without even trying to make landfall at all.

The placenames of Colonsay and Oronsay have many stories to tell and much to give to anyone who may be interested in getting to know them. They are an integral part of these precious islands' unique heritage. It would be an awful pity to forget them.

5
Boys' Ploys

It did not take much to lure me away from my work or domestic responsibilities, notwithstanding the rewards they gave me, but the more I got to find out about the island the more I was tempted to turn my back on the Pottery and Glen Cottage for an hour or several and head off on yet another voyage of discovery.

Was it simply the sheer beauty of the place that would first set the escapist thoughts in motion, the nagging certainty that, good as it was looking out at the beautiful but familiar Scalasaig views, there, a mere birdflight away over the intervening hill, fresh exhilaration was waiting and wondering what had kept you? And it was to the south and south-west corners of the island that I would most often head for my Mother Nature fix: Garvard and the Strand, the tidal reach that separates Colonsay and Oronsay but which unites them when the tide ebbs and the broad and rippled sands between them are exposed, would bring sure and quick relief to my restlessness.

Walk out from where the road ends at the Strand, past the overhanging finger of the 'Hangman's Rock', complete with its visible rope hole, to *Poll Gorm*, 'the blue pool', a true and invitingly swimmable lagoon when the tide is out, that lies between the two islands and where you can sit and take in the stunning views over the eastern mouth of the Strand and across the seas to the Paps of Jura beyond. Or take a longer walk along the Garvard shore, past the islets of the Strand's western entrance, its seabirds, seals, long-abandoned kelp-burning kilns once used to generate sodium carbonate for soap-production and back past Garvard Farm and the standing stone on a tummocky knoll called *Cnoc Eabragainn* ('Dispute resolution hill') where islanders in the age of Norse influence would gather to decide the issues of the day and, on occasion presumably, who should or should not be sent to the Hangman's Rock for summary justice.

On a day with a good spring-tide ebb, when there is a period of two or three hours or so when the Strand can be walked or even driven over (but extremely slowly and mindfully), then a trip to Oronsay might be undertaken. Usually this would be as a special outing with family or friends, for the journey and the place are in a category all of their own. Second only to Iona, Oronsay is an island with a very particular kind of magic that seems to suffuse the senses, just as soon as you have splashed your way through the remnant of the tidal stream that invariably marks the last few yards of the journey before you make proper landfall, at the track that leads to the Priory and is called *An t-aoireadh* ('The worshipping'). Is it merely an effect of the light – from the vast, overarching, more often than not pearl-blue sky, intensified by its reflection in the surrounding sea and sands – that affects the imagination so? Or is it because it is a place now eternally imbued with the resonance of those true saints of the early Celtic church, those intensely spiritual explorers, not least Saint Columba, who built a simple church and then a priory for the successive generations of monks who lived, worked, prayed and died here?

Should you, though, make the mistake, as I once did like others before and since, of treating the tricky drive over at all casually, then you may well find that you now have an unholy extra travelling companion called hubris. The route over is usually fairly well indicated by the furrowed tracks left in the sand by the local vehicles which have business to do on Oronsay. If you stray away from these tracks to the Garvard side, the sand becomes soft enough in many places for a vehicle to sink into and get well and truly stuck. Try to drive across too soon, too late or too speedily, and when there is still too much water lying in the lowest part of the route, and you may stall the car. Either hazard can result in your vehicular pride and joy having to be

abandoned and, if you can't achieve a rescue in time, being submerged between tides before it can be pulled clear: an event
which is guaranteed to leave its driver returning carless, with
dented pride and not nearly enough spiritual compensation.

My own trip with hubris as unexpected passenger occurred
one winter's night after I had driven artist friend, Alasdair
McMorrine, back to his then home at Seal Cottage, a beachside
location which any Hollywood film producer would die for,
or should at least risk making the journey over the Strand to
see. Whether it was the dreamlike quality of the small hour or
the relaxing after-effects of Alasdair's Highland hospitality, I felt
serenely untroubled to be driving back in the moonless dark and
the steady rain, for I knew for certain that the state of the tide was
right for the crossing and I felt a certain Bond-like confidence
in a journey I had made several times before – though not, I
soon realised with adrenalin-laced horror, by the confused route
I had now ended up taking, right into the soft sand which was
trying hard to effect its gloopy grip on the wheels of the heavy
old Hillman and bring it to a stalling standstill. I pressed the foot
down in desperation, driving far too fast over the hard areas of
sand, but only just enough to escape the nightmarish drag of the
quagmire. There was no sign through my flailing windscreen
wipers of any car-tracks I could retrace, except the ones in the
bouncing headlights which I realised that I had just made myself
and was now crossing and re-crossing. I had become completely
disorientated, but kept going till I eventually picked out a rocky
outcrop with hard sand around it where I could safely stop the
car and take stock.

I still had no idea where I had ended up, but by walking out
into the middle of the Strand I eventually saw a distant light,
which had to be Garvard Farmhouse, the home of Donald 'Garvard' and his wife, Joan, better known as 'Pony'. Though I now
had found my bearings, I still had to drive back through patches
of gloop and the fringe of a now rapidly advancing tide before I
could make dry land and wend my way home again, a humbled
but marginally wiser potter, serene now only in the feeling of

utter relief that I had somehow got away with it, car and reputation more or less intact.

But my preferred bolthole, my very favourite place of all the many wonderful and uplifting places in and around Colonsay and Oronsay, was *Ardskenish* (pronounced Ard-skee-nish and derivation unclear, though 'promontory point area' seems possible) a peninsula of wild and isolated perfection that sticks out from the south-west corner of Colonsay into the Atlantic Ocean, and is subject to all its ceaseless attentions and untameable moods. I became smitten the very first time I walked into it with Jane and baby Danny, five months old but already a seasoned backpacker, gurgling contentedly in his carrying frame. Thereafter, I would visit it roughly once a week during our years on the island, whether I had the semblance of an excuse or not – though I was soon to discover some excellent ones – and it delivers, without failing, the same buzz of deep inner pleasure whenever I return to Colonsay. To this day, Ardskenish remains the faithful companion of my dreams and my sometimes sleepless nights, when I will walk its shoreline again in my mind's eye and revisit all its private corners, which I came to know so well.

The quickest way to get to Ardskenish was and is to drive to the golf course on the machaired west side of Colonsay and then walk out across (nowadays around) the airstrip that points westward to the great knob of rock, crowned with an Iron Age fort called *Dun Gallain* (commonly pronounced 'Done Gallon' and meaning the fort of some Viking notable called Gallan, it is suggested) and which looks like the prow of a great galleon bound for eternity to battle the incoming seas. The tractor track from the last gate on the golf course soon leaves the machair and its sea views behind as it climbs gently upwards between the inland knolls, which seem as if they have been put there just to increase the never-failing suspense of waiting to lay one's eyes again on the view just the other side of the approaching ridge.

As you start the descent from the top of the pass known as *Bealach na traigh* (pronounced bell-uch-nuh-try), 'the beach pass', you will usually smell and hear the seas breaking along the shore below before you have got far enough around the last tantalising corner to see them. The panorama which greets you then is one of sumptuous Hebridean majesty: its delicacy and detail magnified by its wildness and grandeur; beaches of cream-coloured sand, a sea of a thousand shades of blue, from translucent Mediterranean turquoises in benign sunshine to bruised purples and brooding greys on less gentle days; white, curling breakers thumping onto menacing black rocks; nosey seals, seabirds bobbing on the swell or wheeling carelessly in the wind, whether gale force or sea breeze; skerry after ever more distant skerry, each eyebrowed white as the swell breaks upon it or tumescing and subsiding as the dark lump of water glides over its form unbroken; the great, consuming sweep of the ocean so huge and alive and spectacular. The long yellow-green arm of Ardskenish stretches out into the distance, its fingers of rock and sand reaching far out into the sea at low water with just the bare knuckles showing when the whole picture is transformed by the flooding tide. All set against a backdrop of the rolling, marram-covered dunes in the foreground, the low-lying islands of Oronsay and Islay across the seas to the south and the overarching infinity of sky above, sometimes azure and sunlit, sometimes full of racing clouds, ever-changing but eternal and magnificent.

That it is a sight to die for I shared with Ross Darroch, one of whose favourite sayings was 'Ach, never died a winter yet!' and, though even he did in the end, the immortal part of this man of legend still lives large in the memories of those that knew him and surely will inhabit Ardskenish till the end of time itself. The day before Ross left the island to join the Army in the Second World War, he decided to take a last walk around this, his very favourite part of Colonsay to take in a final view of the place in all its ineffable glory. On an impulse, he picked up a piece of speckled white quartz and wedged it between two of the striated ledges of the grey rock face from which the tortuously narrow track at *Beulach na Traigh* is hewn. He was wondering whether he would survive the war and see it again; and thinking that, if he did not, it would serve as his memento, known only to himself and the place he loved.

When, thirty years later, Ross stopped to point out the wedged stone and tell me the story behind it, it had become something of a talisman which he always removed and re-wedged for good luck each time he went down to Ardskenish. On this occasion he was taking me to the very end of the peninsula to initiate me into one of his favourite ploys, soon to become one of my own.

The love of the ploy was, and surely still is, embedded deeply in the unreconstructed psyche of every Colonsay male, whether native-born or incomer. The dictionary understands that ploys are 'escapades for the purpose of amusement', though a Colonsay version might also include 'almost always involving the sea and a happy hunting ground'. Ploys, places and favourite people go together and, though they can be enjoyed alone, the better the company the more deeply pleasurable the ploy is almost certain to be. The one that the peerless Ross Darroch was taking me on was to be a cracker, a veritable ploy of ploys, and one upon which I have subsequently expended hours and hours of contented effort and total absorption, whenever the tides and the opportunity have been right.

When Ross came down to the pottery he would often wax lyrical, technical and quite often theatrical about this particular ploy, whetting my appetite for it and the master class and adventure he was now about to give me. He was taking me to the very toe-end of the Ardskenish peninsula to show me holes in the rocks where the lobsters secreted themselves and where, at the lowest of spring tides – and if you knew where the holes were and how to go about it – you should be able to extricate a living lobster or two, or even more if you were very lucky.

We had set out smartly that morning, making sure we would have plenty of time to get to the point of Ardskenish a couple of hours before low water, when access to the lobster holes becomes possible. There was to be an appetiser on the way to this ploy too, another favourite activity of Ross's known as *'shiubhal a' chladaich'* (pronounced 'hew-ul uh chlatt-ich' and meaning 'following/

walking, the shore' but implicitly meaning 'in the hope of finding something worth salvaging en route'). No one derived greater contemplative pleasure or more frequent material reward than Ross from following the tideline and casting his expert eye over what the wide Atlantic had thrown up on far-flung Colonsay's remote shores. He scanned and assessed the jetsam as he walked past it like the master shore-walker he was, stopping only to scrutinise some potential find – a bucket, a brush, a broom handle, a cap, a storm-battered creel, an inflatable plastic float, a solid aluminium one or, still coming ashore in those days, a glass one used by the Spanish fishermen, a tangle of promising-looking rope or twine, a decent piece of timber, sometimes even mahogany or teak, a fragment of a wrecked dinghy with a useful cleat still attached or, perhaps, just as interestingly though less usefully, a clump of black and white goose barnacles which had attached themselves to a piece of driftwood and grown there contentedly on their long voyage up the Gulf stream.

Just occasionally you might come across a sinister-looking cylinder with the words 'Do not touch – inform Royal Navy immediately' written on it, or a plastic current-marker which offered a small reward on return to the scientific body which had released it; and there were always, always wooden and plastic fish-boxes with suppliers' names on them from Peterhead to Maine. The tideline offerings seemed endless, and Ross would decide whether they were worthy of his rescue and re-use. If one was then it would be stashed safely beyond the furthest reach of even the highest storm-driven tide, where it would be collected and carried home in due course. Ross would never return from Ardskenish empty-handed: if it wasn't a day for the lobsters then it would be a day for the shotgun, and the likely result was something for the pot: a rabbit at least and, in the winter months a duck or a barnacle goose if he was in luck. On those exceptional occasions when he wasn't, he would still have a prize or two from the shore, which he referred to as his 'supermarket', to bring home.

We had reached the point of Ardskenish and, from the base of a rock face abutting an ancient raised beach of large boulders which had been smoothed and rounded by the action of a long-departed sea, we retrieved a couple of carefully secreted *cliobs* (pronounced 'cleeps'), which were the hooks which Ross had made out of fence-wire and then attached to the end of the hazel poles we would be using to try to extract the lobsters from their holes, if they were at home. From our vantage-point on the last shelf of heather-clad land we looked down on the area where the action would take place, a confused expanse of rocks and rock pools strewn with glistening, yellow-brown seaweed, bubbled bladderwrack, fronds of flaccid kelp and long thin umber bootlaces floating in the sandy creeks and snaking eerily after the retreating tide. Beyond these lay the grass-topped islets and drying skerries with their recumbent Atlantic seals, whose long, siren-like calls mingled with those of the shriller birdlife: waders, divers, ducks and gulls all busily and noisily going about their business, unfazed by the immensity and restlessness of the vast ocean seascape which embraced the scene.

How on earth would one hope to locate a lobster in this sub-littoral expanse of rock and seaweed, without a boat and a lobster creel? Ross knew and led me down on to the slippery hunting ground to show me where and how. We were looking for deep holes in the exposed rocks close to, at, or sometimes even below, the still-receding tideline. Into these a lobster will retreat and rest; sometimes, it would appear, to harden up a new shell, having cast its old one; more often, it seemed, to wait for the tide or the urge to feed before returning to feed on the seabed. Most of the entrances to the holes were obscured by curtains of seaweed draped over them, which Ross flicked aside and then gingerly inserted his lobster hook into, hoping for the tell-tale clonk and tug that a lobster would angrily give the unwelcome intruder as it locked one of its two claws, the heavy and powerful 'hammer' claw or the lighter and more rapier-like 'pincer' claw, onto the probing wire hook.

At which point battle has commenced, with the lobster, at least initially, refusing to release its vice-like grip; and therefore, if you are gentle, still capable of being eased out of its watery hidey-hole till it emerges, unhappily, into the daylight. There it has to be grabbed instantly and confidently from behind the point where its claw arms join its body, and it must be held so that it cannot lay either of its now antagonised, flailing claws, which it is capable of rotating unexpectedly far back towards you, on the fingers of your grasping hand and giving you the unforgettably traumatic experience of a lifetime. More often than not, however, when the wily crustacean realises it is going to lose the fight with the raider, it lets go of the 'cliob' and reverses smartly back into the hidden depths of its hole. Next time you try to hook it, the lobster may be less keen to engage, and your only way of extracting it will be to get the hook, which is at least a couple of inches wide, in behind its claws and around its body, so that it can be pulled, still slowly and carefully to avoid damaging the creature, out of its lair.

Easier said than done, for lobster holes have rocks, snags, kinks and sometimes secret passages, any of which the lobster can seem to use deliberately to defy and, not infrequently, elude your best attempts at successful extrication. Some of the holes are permanently seafilled from surrounding pools, and the lobster will splash and scuttle backwards into one, hiding remarkable quickly if you are not quick enough to grab them if and when they emerge. Others are under awkward-to-get-at ledges of rock which leave you, the hunter, feeling uncomfortably vulnerable should you reach the point of coming eye to beady eye with a lobster which you have infuriated, and which always looks like an alien, albeit a fascinating, beautiful and, ultimately, particularly delicious alien.

Moreover, if you spend too much time sparring fruitlessly with one resistant lobster, you will be losing the bigger battle with the soon-returning tide and the race to check the other holes you know, which are well dispersed throughout the seaweed-covered hunting ground. If you are lucky, at the end of two or three hours scrambling, slipping and poking about, you will return to the higher ground of Ardskenish, limbs aching, clothes soaked but exhilarated by 'the thrill of the chase', the joy of the ploy and the place and, hopefully, with a lobster or two. Ross and I got four good-sized ones between us that memorable day, and although we never went together again to the Ardskenish lobster holes, as it is really a younger person's activity, I would always give Ross a blow-by-blow account of each trip I subsequently made there, whether to try to hook a lobster or shoot something for the pot, and Ross would pore over the detail and recount and relive his lifetime's successful and one-that-got-away Ardskenish adventures. That he had found someone who shared his enthusiasm for the place and the ploys it offered was a modest return for the matchless gift he gave me too that spring day at the far end of furthest-flung Ardskenish.

The other time-honoured way of making the trip to Ardskenish was by boat and, though this boatless ploy could not have been improved upon, I soon came to learn that boats and ploys were made for each other, and that no man on the island understood or exploited this relationship better than Big Peter or *Para Mor*. Born seaman, surely as skilled as any of his Riasg Buidhe forebears, Peter's preferred and most productive lobster-fishing ground was Ardskenish's maze of skerries and channels which he knew intimately and which he worked, summer through autumn, from his own thirty-foot-long boat, *The Thrive*, with his uncle, Old Peter, acting as crew.

When Old Peter, then in his mid-seventies, became poorly one autumn, Big Peter invited me to substitute till Old Peter recovered. Thus, for a few weeks, I had the privilege at seeing the master at work close up. Like Old Peter I was given responsibility for working the controls and trying to manoeuvre the boat helpfully, while Big Peter, clad in his yellow oilskins and faded white seaboots, pulled the carefully located lobster creels up from the seabed and then reset them, standing forward on the open deck of *The Thrive* with nothing to stop him falling into the ocean other than the fringe of a gunwale no more than three inches in height and his uncanny sense of balance. While the substitute crew was ever so grateful that he had a cockpit to cling to, he would have been quite happy to have had a safety harness as well when the seas turned choppy. Big Peter, by contrast, would look as if he had grown organically from the deck, calmly bending his knees and shifting his weight in reciprocal, almost balletic response to every motion of the boat beneath him, while continuing to handle the creels with minimum effort and maximum expertise, and reading each approaching wave like a page in a book that he pretty well knew off by heart.

When after only a few months living on the island, I was unexpectedly offered the job of 'Assistant Piermaster' – a billing which didn't quite live up to the fact that the ferry only came in three times a week, weather permitting – I became Big Peter's sidekick, not just on the Pier but whenever the need and the opportunity arose for a variety of boating ploys, not least those requiring the measure of additional vim and vigour that a young and enthusiastic gofer was keen to supply.

The gofer's attributes were tested to the full whenever we made the boat trip to Oronsay, at the behest of Andrew ('A.S'. as he was popularly referred to) McNeill who had farmed the island since the early 1950s with his wife, Flora, sister of Donald 'Garvard' and therefore another native '*Orasach*', who kept as hospitable a home as you would ever be likely to find throughout the length and breadth of the Hebrides. A.S. would give Peter a call when the time and the tide looked right to put new sheep on and remove old ones from two neighbouring islets, *Eilean Ghaoidmeal*, 'Islet of the stolen rent' which lay to the east of Oronsay, and *Eilean Nan Ron,* 'Seal Island', which lay to the south. Both of these small islands were inhabited only by the long-nosed Atlantic grey seals which bred there, the black and white barnacle geese which grazed them from autumn till spring, the omnipresent seabirds and A.S.'s hardy but contented sheep.

Transporting them to and from the islands was as straightforward an affair as it ever can be whenever sheep are involved. Big Peter would take his boat into the natural pier of vertical rock on clean white sand on the east side of Oronsay called *Port na h'àth*, the 'Kiln port' by Seal Cottage. There, waiting for us on the rock, would be A.S., his clever and nimble sheepdog 'Pete', at least a dozen small sheep selected for fattening up on the lush, goose-manured pasture of the islets and, more often than not, a treasured friend of A.S.'s who could be relied upon to savour the assorted pleasures of the ploy in prospect.

A particular favourite of Andrew and Flora's was Roddy Mac-Donald from South Uist: Roddy 'Roidean' as he was known in his native island, and who, like Andrew, was a renowned piper, not only in full command of all the classical music of the bagpipe but one with the added gift of making it quite impossible for you not to want to get up and dance to his dance-tunes when he played them at a wedding or ceilidh. Roddy was with us on one such ploy when we managed to squeeze twenty-two wedders, a dog and four anything but undernourished men into the welldeck of the '*bata beag*', the more versatile 'wee boat' which Big Peter had recently bought to replace the veteran *Thrive*. The Plimsoll line was only inches above the water that bright cold February morning, but Peter eased the new boat with his usual absolute assurance through the waves, the tops of which were able to have a good look in on the cargo as we slipped through them into *Caolas Laimrig Mhor,* 'the narrows of the big landing place' on Seal Island, where we climbed ashore and would soon give the wedders their freedom.

We had all brought our shotguns with us, as part of the attraction of the ploy was the chance (decidedly slim given the nature of our cargo and our arrival) of getting a goose or two for the pot. The theory was that, after securing the boat, the enthusiastic gofer would be given five minutes grace to race ahead and try and get a shot at, or at least put up for the others to shoot at, some of the many hundreds of barnacle geese that otherwise grazed on Seal Island entirely undisturbed. It was a plan that remained unrevised, despite regular proof that it had little chance of success because the gofer never had enough time to stalk the ever-wary geese before sheep and sheepdog were released, accompanied by the usual whistles and shouts, including several stentorian ones soon bellowed in my direction, advising that time was short and that we needed to get over to Eilean Ghaoidmeal to take some well-fattened sheep off that island. No goose worthy of the name would not take flight on seeing or hearing such a carnival taking place, and the barnacle goose is just about as carnival-averse as any goose can get.

Having successfully completed part one of the mission, at least insofar as the safe disembarkation of the wedders was concerned, the time would be right for a 'piece' and a refreshment to keep out the cold plus, no doubt, a cheery analysis by the three older men as to how and why the potter had failed to deliver on the goose front. No matter, a cormorant (known locally as a skart and then still popular with the older islanders as an occasional food source) would do instead, and they were far easier to get a shot at than a goose, particularly if you were on a boat and could surprise them as they popped back up to the surface after a dive. For a few minutes on our trip over to Eilean Ghaoidmeal, the graceful 'bata beag' became piratical and warlike, as broadside after buccaneering broadside was released in the general direction of a departing skart, one or two of which would, by the law of averages, succumb to this hostile action and be taken home to end up on some grateful older islander's dinner table.

The biggest challenge lay ahead, however: dealing with the un-sheeplike sheep on Eilean Ghaoidmeal. There were just three sheep on the islet on that occasion, the last survivors of ten that had been bought from a canny man with a huge, red flowing beard that I can still see parting neatly each side of his neck as he battled his way down the pier one stormy day. He was Peter Kelly who farmed Balnahard in the north of Colonsay, and from whom A.S. had purchased them with an eye to fattening up for purely local consumption, as the mutton they would produce after months of living like kings on these rich feeding grounds was ample justification for the effort involved in putting them there and taking them off. The three survivors had, in fact, been living happily there for a couple of years, having eluded the one or two previous attempts to remove them. The reason for their escape soon became clear. They had forgotten they were meant to be domesticated. They had blossomed mentally as well as physically since being given the freedom from human and canine interference that their remote and fertile island fiefdom had provided. They had well-developed horns and attitude to match, a knowing look in their eye and they no longer knew fear of the dog – a fact which Pete had cottoned onto instantly. And they had grown surprisingly big, fat and muscular, with huge fleeces, and were the size, as I see them now, of Shetland ponies.

The three older men and the dog looked on as the gofer was deployed, clutching Big Peter's ten-foot-long boathook, to pursue them individually up, down, across and around the islet's rough terrain, hoping to corner one as it came up against some less easily surmountable natural barrier and get near enough to twist the end of the boathook into its fleece and hold it securely until reinforcements arrived. Even when they did it required a final rugby tackle and the combined efforts of the menfolk to haul one of the creatures from the point of capture to the boat. There was much pulling and heavy lifting, there was slipping and cursing in two languages, there were clouds of steam rising from the crimson-faced gofer and there was a sense of huge relief and no small triumph as we eventually loaded two of these magnificent specimens into the boat, having left the last, proudest and most elusive of the Mohicans to live to fight another day in the wild and beautiful redoubt that it now ruled alone and, till the next visit, whenever that would be, undisturbed.

'Ach well, Potter, it's a pity you weren't up for the third one,' Peter teased mercilessly as we chugged back contentedly to *Port na h-àth* on the Oronsay shore with our resigned cargo. 'And I doubt that boathook will ever be the same again,' he added as a sense of great good humour suffused the ship's company, though the two captured sheep still looked a bit miffed. The contents of more than one hip flask did the rounds, the stories flowed too and the magic of the place and of the moment settled upon us timelessly. This was the deep joy of the perfect ploy, but if some nevertheless, still unsatisfied, part of you might still be looking for icing on the cake, then A.S. would deliver it to your door a few days later, in the form of the best lamb dressed as mutton that you would ever be lucky enough to savour.

6

BIRDS OF PARADISE

No ploy gave me such an instant and readily accessible buzz, however, as the island's birdlife – so prolific, busy and vital that it felt as if one was entering the birds' world and not the other way around. They were everywhere and full of variety; in look, call, habit and habitat, and it soon became a hobby and source of unfailing solace to watch them and get to know them as they went about their business, sometimes, it has to be admitted, at the expense of my own.

It was just too tempting, when I could see from the pottery door that the tidal conditions would be right, not to make a spur of the moment executive decision to desert the workplace and nip off in the car to a favourite birdwatching spot, like the Strand road end, just to see what was doing. Using the car as a moveable and comfy bird hide, I would sit in the parking place and scan the steadily advancing line of the tide's edge for familiar and occasionally unfamiliar wading birds: the cheery and noisy oystercatchers, over-anxious redshanks and wheepling curlews, often with their smaller, straight-billed cousins, the bar-tailed godwits, alongside. Still smaller regulars included dunlin and ringed plover, and occasionally, in winter, small flocks of white sanderling scuttling backwards and forwards along the edge of the advancing tide on their electrically charged legs. Every now and then, and with a mix of thrill and anxiety lest it fly away before I had been able to identify it, I would encounter something new and exciting, like a grey plover with its characteristic black oxter, or small groups of the coffee-brown-black and disconcertingly duck-sized Brent geese, pausing for a feed before resuming their journey to Ireland, since they did not overwinter in either Colonsay or Oronsay.

Many other geese did though: in particular, the strikingly black, white and delicately grey-rippled barnacle geese which, in the first weeks of October, make their heroic migratory journey back from their Icelandic breeding grounds to their winter feeding areas. Several hundred base themselves on Seal Island and neighbouring Oronsay and graze mainly there and at Ardskenish until they make their return journey at the beginning of May to breed. A much smaller number of grey geese – greylags and whitefronts – also wintered on Colonsay, the greylags preferring the big farm fields of Kiloran in the sheltered heart of the island, the whitefronts the isolated and much more secluded pastures of Ardskenish.

Of all the island birding events that anyone may witness, whether confirmed birdwatcher or casual passerby, surely none is so soul-stirring and evocative as the return of the geese in the autumn, and it was notable how every islander made a point of sharing the news when they had heard the first of them: the pink-feet, which passed high overhead night and day in late September on their journeys even further afield. The skin-prickling significance of their reappearance was felt by everyone: summer was over and the long months of winter lay ahead.

During one autumn, I had joined a cross-section of Colonsay manhood, all hired on a short-term contract by Argyll County Council to provide a few weeks fairly well-paid labour helping to resurface a section of the island's single-track road network, which that year included tarmacking the road across the golf course to the airstrip at Machrins. Our squad was under the 'let's be having none of your nonsense' command of Jasper Brown, the senior of the island's two roadmen, a star of a man who also had the distinction of having concocted a connoisseur's collection of the most creative set of oaths that I have ever come across. They were mostly in Gaelic, although a Gaelic-English combo was freely used where it enhanced the imaginative force – the tamest of which could be translated as 'Ach, your cojones on toast!'

For the duration of one early October day, as the wind blew a steady near-gale out of the south west and huge waves crashed, roared and crumped along the coastline next to us, we watched in ever-increasing awe and admiration as skein after skein after skein of geese – mostly barnacle but there were plenty of greylag and whitefronts too – arrived from the north-west. Some came in near-perfect V-formations with their leading birds dropping back to let another take over lead position with an almost regimental precision. Others came in low over the waves looking battle-wearied and ragged, though still working hard to re-group and calling noisily to lone stragglers who were surely entitled to feel exhausted after their unbroken thousand-mile-plus journey with nothing in sight but a boundless, heaving ocean by day and, by night, such stars as weren't hidden by storm-driven clouds.

We must have seen many thousands of geese that October day, passing over us before seeming to readjust their flightpaths to a more southerly direction. A small minority of them would settle, no doubt gratefully, on nearby Oronsay and Seal Island, but most would be following a course to Islay and beyond. Flights would continue to pass overhead for the next few days and nights, but in quickly decreasing numbers until the finality of the seasonal change was established and bird, beast and human had adjusted their lives to the rapidly shortening days and long nights of autumn and the approaching winter.

Though sea-girt Colonsay only rarely experienced the frost and snows of the distant Highland landmass, the island felt the full, unmitigated force of the gales and storms, sometimes of full hurricane strength, that swept in off the Atlantic, more often than not with an accompaniment of horizontal rain, sleet or vicious hail. On a clear, calm day, with the sun shining, often surprisingly warmly, and the sea sparkling silver, winter in Colonsay becomes benign and most beautiful, but as it lingered on and on, one would come to ache for the first signs of a new spring and long for the return of the first of the summer migrants.

The very earliest of these returners is the dapper wheatear, called 'the little stonemason', *clacharan* in Gaelic, because its short 'check-check' noise resembled the sound of a mason's hammer at work, a noise that can be mimicked by skyting a couple of round stones off each other. The first wheatears return from Africa to the island's machair as early as the middle of March, the advance guard for the main invasion of spring migrants which starts some weeks later. In the third and fourth weeks of April you will start to notice the wistful and so-good-to-hear-again song of the willow warbler, the familiar call of the cuckoo and the shrill and insistent piping of the common sandpipers as they advertise for mates and mark out their territories all along Colonsay's shores. The first sighting of sweeping swallows is another welcome sign that spring has arrived, though it is not until late May, when the few well-wintered geese that still remain have left for their Arctic summer homes again, that one spots the last of the migrants, like the whitethroat singing from the top of its favourite bramble bush in the Glassard glen, and whose presence really does confirm that early summer has finally arrived.

In late May and early June, when breeding birds are at their twenty-four seven busiest, the short twilight nights are particularly noisy. The resident snipe drum and rasp, the migrant sedge and grasshopper warblers chatter and reel respectively and then, just as you were about to nod off again, comes the grating, almost mechanical, 'creck-creck' call of the corncrake.

Islanders would aver that the noise had driven more than one sleepless crofter to reach under the bed for the twelve-bore and burst out into the night to discharge it dementedly in the general direction of the feathered offender, albeit without any chance whatsoever of silencing a bird that conceals its location so effectively by hiding in the longest grass and by throwing its voice better than a trained ventriloquist. However, nothing could explain the strangest of night-time noises we heard during our first two summers in Glen Cottage though never again after that, a churring, whirring sound, coming and going. Our neighbour up the hill, Mary Clark, explained that it was the bird the islanders called the '*cuidheal mhor*', 'the big wheel', because the nightjar's call resembled nothing so much as the sound of a revolving cartwheel, so those who had named it believed.

Nowhere is Colonsay springtime's world of birds busier or more truly spectacular than at *Aoineadh nam Muc,* the 'Pigs' Terrace' or 'Pigs' Paradise' as it is popularly known. Behind and beyond the stretch of high moorland that separates the crofts of Kilchattan from the western ocean lie cliffs which rise to nearly 400 feet from the rocky shore below. Though it is possible to pick a safe way to walk in from a southerly direction to the base of the precipitous 'Pigs' Paradise' section of the cliffs, care and caution are the watchwords, and the best view is to be had from the sea – on a decent day for small boats and their seafarers. There in May you will discover a seething, deafening and pungent skyscraper metropolis, home to what seems like at least a million jostling, bickering and screaming black and white seabirds, flying ceaselessly to and from the calmer seas beyond and below in search of food for their fledglings or even, perhaps, just to get five minutes break from the relentless drama and hubbub of their dangerously overcrowded lodgings. Fulmars, kittiwakes, guillemots, razorbills, crested shags and cormorants amongst others all compete for their miniscule slices of real estate on the cliff-face ledges, some providing barely enough room to lay an egg. If you're very lucky you may also spot a bullying 'bonxie', the great skua, or a high-speed peregrine giving one of the infinite crowd below its professional attentions. It is all just as glorious nature intended, and a sight well worth the seeing.

But of all the island's rich variety of wonderful birds, from familiar garden favourites to those which have become niche specialists in the unique island environment, none gave me a greater thrill of personal discovery, or still gives me such unfailing pleasure, as the chough – a rare member of the crow family that is found in only a few of the remoter western outposts of the British Isles. With its jet-black plumage, glinting iridescent bottle-green in the sunlight, its intensely orange-red bill and carmine legs, it makes a most dramatic fashion statement whenever you may be lucky enough to see it up close. You may also gasp in wonderment at the brilliance of its aerobatics as it twists, turns and flips its flightpath at the last possible moment, primary feathers fully extended like splayed fingers on a black, outstretched hand, hurtling recklessly over a cliff edge, somehow avoiding the endless streams of commuting gulls and guillemots, and then, with a final flick and flourish, vanishing in less than a blink of an eye into some deep and inaccessible fissure in the cliff face where it has its nest. But it is the chough's unique, unmistakeable call – an electrifying, ecstatic cry, a pulse of raw energy that sends a shiver down the spine – which epitomises its character, sets it apart and makes it, for me, the most exciting and iconic of all Colonsay's wonderful birds.

It has had a chequered island history, however. It was once so common on Colonsay at the end of the nineteenth century that, according to the author Gathorne Hardy, it used to be shot and made into chough pie! It seems unlikely, however, that shooting alone would have been the sole cause for its subsequent decline and complete disappearance from Colonsay and Oronsay by the middle of the twentieth century. Its rediscovery in the early 1970s was due to an outstanding north country birdwatcher called Reg May, who used to come and stay with John Clark and his mother Effie at Scalasaig Farm in the late spring. He found the first pair to nest again in a remote and inaccessible cliff face north of Kiloran Bay, and each year since then it has continued to prosper, so that forty years later it is such a pleasingly common sight in most parts of both Colonsay and Oronsay.

In the twenty-first century, when the interests of the island's birdlife are carefully watched over by the RSPB who have owned Oronsay since 1996, it may seem retrogressive to recall that islanders traditionally made good use of the island's natural food supply, not least that provided by some of the birds and their eggs. In the 1970s, most of the male islanders owned a shotgun which they would use mainly to try to pulverise clay pigeons at the regular shooting matches held at the edge of Machrins Bay. Some would also use them to shoot the occasional rabbit, and a few, myself included, would also enjoy the much less straightforward challenge of trying to pot a duck or a goose in which the islands also abounded. Geese would usually be painstakingly stalked, by crawling and slithering along drainage ditches and behind stone dykes, trying to get within range unless the ever-alert geese sensed you first, which they all too often did, and then your sole reward would be their noisy and spectacular taking to the skies. We always seemed to have a goose for Christmas dinner, though.

Ducks were even harder to stalk, and the favoured method in Colonsay and Oronsay was to head out early evening before the sun went down to one of the favoured shallow pools that were formed by the autumn and winter rains on the machair, and take cover behind a stone dyke as the daylight dwindled away, listening hyperintently for the telltale rush of wings as the mallard, wigeon or teal flew in to take up their overnight accommodation. Once they had settled and if it wasn't too dark by then you might be lucky to get a clean shot and return home with something for the table. More often than not, though, the light would fade too far or the ducks had chosen another pool to visit. Then what you were left with was the meditative experience of sitting outside in perfect stillness as night fell, your senses nourishing themselves on the smell and the feel of the wind, the close-of-play calls of familiar birds near and far and, soon, as the cold seeped into your stiffening limbs, the sight of night clouds drifting over the face of the moon, or of the stars appearing like fairy lights in their vast overhead canopy until, eventually, you came to and realised it was high time you were heading home to the warmth of your family, with or without something for another day's dinner.

The annual cull exacted by island residents was minimal, and every bird and rabbit shot was cooked and enjoyed by an island household, with any surplus to the shooter's personal requirements invariably passed on to grateful older neighbours in particular, who had grown up with such fare as part of their staple diet. A small handful of older islanders still gathered and ate the eggs of wild birds as they came into season, starting with the lapwings which began laying at the end of March, and followed by the gulls and ducks in the succeeding months. Neither form of harvesting ever appeared to make any impression on the abundance of targeted birds.

Nevertheless, while the potter would readily skive off to become an enthusiastic hunter bent on bringing something home for the pot, his many wild-goose chases only increased his appreciation of their way of life. So much so that, in time, he too came to adopt the conclusion that a much wiser islander and more experienced shot had reached about the whole wild-fowling business, the attractions of which he had savoured in full since his boyhood days growing up on Oronsay. 'Well, they are such wonderful creatures, Potter, that I just don't seem to have the heart any more,' Donald 'Garvard' once said to me, quite non-judgementally, for that was not the way of a man whose special gift it was to always leave anyone who came into his company feeling more whole and happier. Donald was right, the birds of Colonsay and Oronsay are truly marvellous; an integral and expressive part of a superlative natural environment and constant companions in the island way of life which Donald, also a Colonsay bard most worthy of the name, commemorates in his Gaelic poem, *An T-Iasgair, (Togail nan cliabh)* 'The Fisherman (Lifting the Creels)'.

Light is my step as I head for the boat,
The skylark is joyously greeting the day.
If I get underway at the height of the tide,
The current will lift her and take her away.
Many's the sight I have seen when at sea:
Small seals, just like sheep, on the rocks fast asleep,
Black skarts, superb fishermen, probing the waves
And the kittiwakes taking me back to my youth.
As a boy I would often climb up those cliff paths,
To hunt for their eggs with my heart pounding hard,
My toes in a crack, holding on by my nails,
The screaming of seagulls just filling my ears,
A faithful black guillemot always close by,

Carefully working to gather its food,
And like a star falling that sparkles with gold,
The gannet comes splashing right into the sea.
In *Caolas na Cailliche* the tide runs just fine,
Dubh Hirteach lighthouse stands guard in the west,
If I line up the *Dubh-sgeir* with Ben Riach's cairn,
I'll not be left wanting when I lift up my creel,
Though the clouds may drive in, the heavens grow dark,
And the foam off the waves splash onto the sail,
I'll not have a care unless a rope goes,
For the sounds all around are a choir to my ears.

Gur aotrom mo cheum-sa mi deanadh gu bàt'
An uiseag gu sunndach cur failt' air an là.
Ma gheibh mi fo astar ri airde muir'-làin,
Thig buille 'san t-ruth chuireas siubhal 'na sàil.
Gur iomadach sealladh a chi mi air cuan:
Roin bheaga mar chaoraich air creig's iad'nan suain;
Sgarbh dubh, an sar-iasgair, a sgrudadh 'sna tuinn,
Is sgàireag na creig a' toirt m'oige 'nam chumn'.
Gur tric's 'nam bhalach a streap mi na dreis,
A' rurach a h-uighean. 's mo chridhe air leum,
Mo ladhran am fruchag, is m'ingnean an greim,
Sgreid fhaoileann a' lionadh mo chlaisteachd gu leir.
Tha callag bheag dhileas bhios daonnan 'nam chomhair,
Gu faiceallach, dicheallach trusadh a lon.
Mar rionnag a' tuiteam, 's i dearrsadh mar or,
Le spairt air an uisg' thig an t-eun-sgadain mor.
Ann an Caolas na Cailliche bidh sruth mar as miann,
An Dubh Hirteach 'na sheasadh air faire 'san iar.
Ma gheibh mi ans Dubh-sgeir air carn Beinn Riabhach,
Cha bhi mise falamh mar thogas nan cliabh.
Ged thig dubhadh air speuran le iomairt nan neòil,
Is sioban thar thonnan a' fhliuchas an seòl,
Cha bhi mi fo churam ma sheasas na ròp;
'Se choisir 'nam chluais a bhith 'geisdachd an ceòil.

7

LET THERE BE LIGHT

It was never the most riveting of names to conjure with, but the Glassard and Scalasaig Tenants Electricity Association served a useful purpose in its day and, in the process, took an off-duty potter on another voyage of personal discovery.

Within a few weeks of taking up residence in Glen Cottage I found that I had been imperceptibly coerced by Big Peter, that grandmaster of persuasion, into accepting what he suggested was the almost inconsequential responsibility of becoming the Association's secretary. 'Ach, just in case we need to write the odd letter, Potter, it would be a pity to waste that education of yours,' Peter stated with a disconcertingly knowing twinkle in his eye, ignoring the ex-art student's laments about his lack of academic achievement and somehow forgetting to mention too that, traditionally, the secretary did the treasurer's job as well. My nomination, it later transpired, had been wholeheartedly endorsed by the three other stalwart members of the Association's depleted committee, each of whom had privately made it quite clear to Big Peter that they couldn't possibly find the time to take on the position. Unsurprisingly, the nomination/selection had been unanimously agreed in advance by the four conspirators.

There was no National Grid supply to this tiny, remote and forgotten Hebridean island, which meant that any electrical power had to be of the DIY variety, produced by diesel generators. Colonsay Estate had installed a number of these many years previously in the island's main settlements; and in the biggest one, Scalasaig combined with neighbouring Glassard, they had handed over the ownership and the responsibility of maintaining and managing the supply to the local residents.

The community involved comprised about twenty permanently occupied homes, half of them pensioner households, plus another half dozen or so holiday houses. With the addition of a few other properties like the Doctor's surgery and the farm steadings, there were about thirty buildings which were connected, over the length of meandering mile or so, to an ageing 15 kilowatt diesel generator. It could be switched to another smaller 6 kilowatt veteran and the pair of them spent their declining years living side by side in a dark and oily roadside shed, glorying in the name of the 'power house', a little way below the Church of Scotland manse.

It was a fitting location for an enterprise which had to be run on a wing and a prayer, for the operational challenges were considerable. The additional transport costs meant the price of diesel or petrol was already much higher than the mainland norm by the time it had been shipped to Colonsay, but a further round of freight charges was then levied by the ferry company that brought the fuel over in big, heavy barrels that were deposited on the pier prior to being manhandled to their point of use. Moreover, on top of the resulting record fuel costs were those of replacing exhausted parts, minor and major, from the lion-hearted but worn-out generators. Despite the savings made by the islanders' supreme recycling skills, machine maintenance know-how and the entirely voluntary work that kept the electricity scheme functioning, the Association still had to charge its local customers 10 pence (which would equate to 75p in 2017 prices) for every unit of electricity they used, in order to cover the basic running costs and have just enough in the kitty for spare parts.

To add insult to the long-suffering islanders' injury, the eye-watering cost to the consumer was for very limited usage. The output from the generator was so small if distributed equitably amongst all the regular users, that households were expected to use it for lighting and not much else, with a complete ban applied to the use of electric kettles or other similarly greedy appliances. Although washing-machine use was permitted in daylight morning hours, the generators would be turned off for lengthy periods during the day and late at night to try to reduce expenditure on unnecessary fuel costs. Tilley lamps, torches and candles were kept to hand and used by every local household, therefore, whenever the needs arose – as they were on a regular basis.

That power failures occurred no more frequently than they did was due to one unflappable man, Big Peter, who quietly and unhurriedly kept as watchful and understanding an eye on the two 'jennies' as he did on most other aspects of Colonsay life, not least those that lesser mortals would find an excuse to shy away from. He visited them at least twice daily, he cranked their diesel engines into life, he fuelled them, tended them, operated on them, nursed them, brought them back to health and generally encouraged them to give a great deal more service than their designers could ever, in their wildest dreams, have envisaged.

When the system did come to a sudden, but somehow always still surprising, halt, everyone looked to Big Peter for the solution, and I soon came to understand that part of my unwritten contract as Secretary and Treasurer to the Glassard and Scalasaig Tenants Electricity Association was not simply to turn Peter's meter-readings into bills for which I was then responsible for chasing up payment, but to lend its committed Chairman a hand whenever the lights went out. Had the generators been made out of clay I might have been capable of providing some technical assistance but, irredeemably useless as I was at most matters electrical and mechanical, I was still good for humphing and holding a set of the GPO's best extendable ladders which, as he was also the island's telephone engineer, Peter put to good community use whenever the need arose.

There were some conspiracy theorists in the community who, whenever the supply failed, would wave a speculatively accusing finger at the island's doctor, Andrew Hall-Gardiner, for overloading the system, on the grounds that the lights in his house and surgery always seemed to be blazing, and that he had once been observed in a shop in Oban looking longingly at forbidden items like electric drills. However, the case against him remained stubbornly unproven, and despite the community-spirited efforts of the accusers in, so it was implied, watching telly in the dark and turning the lights out after themselves when they went from room to room, blackouts still occurred; the main reason being a dead short caused by a ferocious gust of wind springing an exposed outside connection. Our job then was to go from pole to pole and building to building inspecting every external connection, until we spotted the fault, usually by torchlight. Big Peter would be in his GPO donkey jacket or yellow oilskins at the business end of the ladder, the potter securing the bottom end, pointing a torch helpfully and otherwise showing solidarity in a resigned and generally dampish sort of way.

It was not an entirely unsociable activity, however. While we always hoped for a quick fix, on more than one occasion we inspected every outside connection on the line starting at the very furthest away house in Glassard and terminating at the other end of the line at Scalasaig Farmhouse, and though we conveyed only the news of failure thus far to every household we passed, they would offer a traditional mix of cheery encouragement and Highland hospitality. Though the temptation was great to sit by a fireside and have a nice cup of tea or something stronger, Peter would generally maintain a steady and unbroken momentum until the fault was finally found and rectified, albeit in the certain knowledge that Effie Clark at our ultimate port of call would invariably welcome us into her farmhouse kitchen, where the best of home baking, hot tea and a rewarding dram would be laid out for us.

Everyone could see that we were fighting a losing battle, and that we had to come up with a more radical and permanent solution to the electricity supply problems. Matters came to a head in the winter of 1975–76 when the big generator's even bigger heart gave out and we were compelled to address the reality we had hoped to avoid. We managed to make an emergency arrangement with Colonsay Estate to plug into the Hotel's generator for the winter, knowing that come the start of the holiday season we would be on our own again. Where should we turn for help? The North of Scotland Hydro Electricity Board, the 'Hydro' as it was universally known, which had drawn its power from the Highland glens they had dammed on a promise of bringing electricity to every community in its service area, no matter how remote or difficult? The Highlands and Islands Development Board (HIDB) whose remit was based on helping disadvantaged communities like Colonsay? At last the Association's Secretary would have some real letters to write instead of those wretchedly expensive electricity bills he had to send out to his neighbours for the privilege of turning on a light bulb or two, and paying five times as much as their mainland counterparts for the privilege.

The NOSHEB response had all the warmth of a midwinter power failure – they just didn't want to know – although they did eventually come to see, as well as deliver, the light. All hope now rested on the HIDB who, though one could sense them taking a very deep breath first, soon showed us they were on our side, and made it clear they wanted to work with us to find a good solution. Although we were only too happy to take them at their word, we could not entirely rid ourselves of the scepticism, turning to cynicism, that can become infectious in small and isolated communities who feel, usually with some justification, that the powers that be are pretty happy to forget about them and let them stew in their own juice – or, in our case, the lack of it.

Little did we guess what new challenges would now come to us, or we might have been tempted to retreat into our comfort zone, even a less well-lit one. Instead we took that first, heavy step forward into the unknown, and became engaged in a very demanding community development project involving a process which I would eventually come to understand much better, but was then experiencing personally and sometimes painfully for the first time. It involves hope, false starts, a steep learning curve, tensions, compromises, the testing and bruising of various egos not least your own, moans and laughter. It should, in all likelihood, if you stick at it, in the fullness of time and it might even be years later, deliver a tangible, practical result more or less along the lines you were hoping for; and bringing with it, almost imperceptibly, a sense of achievement, coupled with one of sheer relief that you don't have to go through it all again, even though you may be surprised to discover that you are much better equipped by your experience to do so next time round.

The deal we eventually worked out with David Henderson, the resolute HIDB economist and piggy-in-the-middle who took on the daunting job of developing and brokering a workable project, had four main elements: setting up and running a community-owned and controlled company called the Colonsay Community Electricity Association, to which the Glassard and Scalasaig forerunner gratefully ceded its responsibilities; a further commitment by the community to not only contribute £1000 for connection fees, but voluntarily to build a brand-new power house for the west side of the island; HIDB funding for all the capital costs of the big new diesel generators and the network of new poles and powerlines which would serve both halves of the island; and, last but never least, the commitment by the Army to install the lot, free of charge, as a training exercise!

The stiffest challenge for the community was surely going to be building the new power house to be sited on a roadside piece of Archie McConnell's croft in Kilchattan. It was not that the islanders would not readily pull together in heart-warming and spontaneous fashion in both fun times and sad; but would local politics prevail, and excuses be found for avoiding the commitments they had given for what still seemed to many a rather suspect experiment in compulsory community cooperation? There was no need to worry unduly, for the early summer sun shone encouragingly and almost unfailingly on the motley crew of locals who turned out over the next few weeks. The piermaster, the estate worker, the roadman, the fisherman, the farmer, the crofter, the odd job man, the schoolbus and digger drivers, the young local home on leave, the painter, the potter and the postie were all among those who laboured away during those May and June weekends and evenings, though not without pausing to pass tart but always humorous comment on any fit male islander who had the temerity to drive past and give the traditional friendly wave to those who were there grafting away on construction. As for the island's connection premium, the very first person on the island to hand in his contribution to the Association's Treasurer was old Ross, who headed straight for the pottery after collecting his pension from the post office.

The real tensions surfaced in the meetings of the new Community Electricity Association, and centred on the burden of costs as well as responsibilities that the community would be left to shoulder after the scheme's backers had reverted to dealing with their mainland priorities. The unit price, the HIDB argued, would have to be 15p a unit (£1.12p per unit would be the 2017 equivalent) but that would mean, we cried in outrage, charging people half as much again as the old Electricity Association did. No, we were told, the 'Hydro' would not give us a subsidy, nor would the local authority and nor would HIDB, despite the fact that the rest of the world was only paying 2p a unit, hadn't had to contribute an additional connection fee nor then build a power house free of charge. We resented the injustice, we didn't like being patronised and we didn't know what more we could do about it. As if this wasn't testing enough, we were now responsible for recruiting and deciding how much to pay someone to look after the newly installed system. To cap it all, we knew only too well that every difficult decision we took at one of our endless evening meetings would be headline news in next day's *Colonsay Gazette* and subject to forensic dissection and sniffs of Hebridean derision from some of the more critical members of the community we were part of. So this is what it felt like trying to take grown-up community responsibility for something that truly affected all our shared lives.

It was a painfully instructive learning curve and a lot to ask, so we fell out, we reverted to type, we retired to the pub to moan some more and drown our sorrows; but, funnily enough, we soon regained our composure and good humour and then got on again as before with our essentially companionable community lives. The fundamental inequity would not be relieved until 1983, when Colonsay was at last connected to the National Grid and households in the community were serviced and charged the same as everyone else who were long used to taking this privilege for granted. There was a flurry of publicity and the *Oban Times* captured the local reaction perfectly in a comment by my old neighbour, Finlay, 'This is the greatest thing that has ever happened. I think the Eskimos had electricity before we did!', adding that his wife, Catriona, had just bought an electric blanket. But as a footnote perhaps in Colonsay's social history, it is still worth recalling the role of the two community-run electricity associations which provided the stepping stones to a much more sustainable way of life in the Colonsay of today.

As for the man who was then a practising potter, another light had gone on which would eventually draw him away from his ceramics, the island which was educating him, and to other kinds of community development projects in pastures new.

8

THE SENSE OF COMMUNITY

If strength and sense of community are determined by the extent to which its members come together and share their daily lives, small and remote islands like Colonsay must be in a league of their own – and if companionable conversation is their common currency, then 1970s Colonsay was not only very well off but generous to a fault.

The 120 or so permanent residents shared a small, bewitching but economically and, in some but most definitely not all aspects, socially disadvantaged community. It relied almost entirely for its subsistence on the arrival, after a two and a half hour journey, of a Caledonian MacBrayne ferry which, when not delayed or cancelled by stormy weather, called three times a week to set down and pick up travellers and to offload the supplies that were essential for the island's survival. And where islanders are drawn together by the very nature of their shared dependencies, they will rarely pass up the opportunity for a bit of companionable socialising.

It is little wonder, then, that, given half decent weather, a large slice of the local population would foregather on the head of the pier, often crowded into its concrete shed to escape the weather, to watch the boat come in: some with business to transact, a delivery to collect, an important journey to make to the mainland, a family member or visitor to welcome or say a fond farewell to. But it almost seemed too as if the islanders had assembled to pay collective witness to what set them apart as a community and made them so distinct from even similar rural mainland ones, which take for granted their much more straightforward access to neighbouring settlements and service centres. In truth, the islanders gathered mainly for the conversational 'craic' and the buzz of satisfaction which the live theatre of the ferry arrival provided, watching from the very front row the ritual raising of the gangplank and disembarkation of assorted people, cars and freight. The comings and goings were keenly observed, not least the safe arrival of the island's mails and supplies, and the appreciative audience maintained a bubbling flow of spontaneous and friendly chatter as the then thrice-weekly drama was enacted.

The sight of the crowd on the pier, whether at basic wintertime levels or swelled by enthusiastic summer visitors, makes a deep impression on the ferry passenger as he or she gazes down, with unconcealed curiosity, from the boat deck onto the colourful mix of people waiting and watching on the quayside below. For those returning home, the sight of the familiar figures and faces as the ferry makes its slow, final approach alongside, is deeply reassuring. For those who have yet to get to know the place, the evidence offered by the scurrying hustle and bustle of the pier and by the interplay of its cast of assorted characters suggests an intriguingly different kind of community, which nevertheless goes about its unfamiliar, small island business in an agreeably human and selfassured way.

But when the ferry has set course for the mainland again and the seagulls have reclaimed their territory on the once more deserted pier, a first-time visitor left behind might well wonder what on earth had become of the lively community, no sooner glimpsed than apparently vanished into thin air. The reality was that while some of its members would have gravitated to the shop to pick up a fresh loaf and others to the pub for a post-ferry analysis and recuperative refreshment, most would have dispersed again to their respective corners of the island to resume their independent lives and responsibilities.

Yet, so the passing weeks and months of a Colonsay year would reveal, the communal life of the islanders was essential to its sense of well-being, and it was woven together, not only by such focal points as the ferry arrival, a visit to the shop, the post office or even the pottery, but by an island-wide web of innumerable, interconnected conversations, and a hidden catalogue of organised gatherings that many bigger communities might envy.

There were ploughing and clay-pigeon shooting matches, a sheep-shearing competition, a sports day, a fun day and a harvest festival called the Root and Grain Show. There were beetle and whist drives, football games, dinner dances, concerts and ceilidhs. There were two functioning protestant churches, Baptist and Church of Scotland, with their different congregations; a Women's Guild and a WRI There were funerals, occasional weddings and 21st birthday parties to which every islander was automatically invited. There was a playgroup, a primary school, a school club, an Easter picnic, a Christmas party and evening classes. There was a Community Council, a Resident's Association and a Hall Committee. There were invariably well-attended volunteer coastguard and fire service groups, and there was always the ever-revolving hub of the pub, the bar at the island hotel, to which the selfsame volunteers would traditionally retire after they had been rehearsed in their evening drills by the visiting Coastguard or Fire Officer and then paid a small but eminently recyclable allowance for the voluntary commitment they had so willingly just demonstrated.

There were tattie-picking days at Scalasaig and Machrins Farms, when schoolchildren, pensioners and those in between would spend a day in a field lifting and bagging the potatoes and laying the surplus in a shallow storage pit called a *'slochd'*, 'gully', where they would be bedded down and covered with straw before being covered by earth to protect them from winter frosts. The rewards for these days were the unceasing 'craic' of the shared ploy, followed by a communal sit-down tea in the farmhouse kitchen, a huge bag of potatoes to keep you going through the winter and, for the aspiring language learner, a rare opportunity to attune an Anglo-Saxon ear to the constant chatter and banter in Gaelic, with even the children forgetting their inhibitions and joining in. How I wish that such daily language immersion could somehow become the norm again!

There were 'puffer' days too when the coal boat, no longer steam-powered but otherwise an easily recognisable offspring of Para Handy's *Vital Spark* would arrive, heavy laden, to tie up alongside the pier. Every available tractor and trailer on the island would be pressed into service to collect the coal, which was offloaded from the cargo boat's hold by a huge, clawed grab that would be swung skilfully on its derrick by the skipper and released with a cascading clatter and crunch into whichever of the assortment of crofters and farmers' trailers was first in the line. Every house in Colonsay and Oronsay would then receive a personal delivery of a ton or two of coal, the deliverer would have a reciprocal offer of (Highland) hospitality and whatever coal remained on board thereafter would be tipped into the 'coal ree' next door to Glen Cottage, to keep the community going till the next time the puffer called.

The ceaseless to-ing and fro-ing of the tractors and trailers was a small boy's dream, whether he was disguised as a participating grown-up or was the genuine article, watching red-haired and wide-eyed through Glen Cottage's garden fence, and exchanging warm smiles and big waves with every single passing tractor driver for as long, it seemed, as the excitement lasted. Equally compelling to the household's small children were those cyclical days in the island year when the same farmers and crofters drove their sheep or their cattle down the Hotel brae and into the holding pens opposite the cottage, where the poor creatures would have to wait overnight, complaining noisily and ceaselessly, until they had been communally cajoled, coerced and even occasionally cursed by their owners, pier-hands and ferry crew, fellow travellers and sheepdogs, into the hold of the next day's ferry for their one-way trip to a livestock sale on the mainland.

Though agriculture had been in steady decline since its nineteenth-century heyday, when Colonsay's famous black cattle and boatloads of farm produce were exported to the mainland, livestock production was still a mainstay of island life, and the farmers and crofters would come together regularly to help each other out when seasonal tasks like dipping, dosing and shearing would benefit from some labour-sharing. They were also originally responsible for creating an island entertainments committee, which went under the *nom de plume* of the Colonsay and Oronsay Young Farmers Club. It was soon made clear, however, that you didn't have to be a farmer, crofter, a relative of same or even in anything like your first flush of youth to become a member and so, on that relaxed basis, a not entirely youthless potter and his genuinely youthful wife were added to the membership list.

Club meetings usually took place in the kitchen of Machrins Farmhouse in the mid-west of the island, where Jessie McNeill dispensed traditional hospitality with her quintessential Hebridean grace, good humour and kindliness. The warmth of Jessie's welcome was only matched by the realisation that the organisation had the kind of laid-back approach that would appeal to anyone with horizontal tendencies, whether native-born or incomer. Meetings had a disarmingly apologetic approach to the business at hand, preferring to come to it long after everyone had arrived, paid visits to the sitting room to say hello to 'Old Roger', Jessie's father, been fed several cups of tea and lovingly prepared accompaniments by Jessie, exchanged and pondered the latest island news, never in short supply, and waited for someone to have the nerve or bad manners to break the spell.

Like an introductory prayer at a routine funeral, the proceedings would eventually begin with the minutes of the last meeting being read out aloud as a salutary reminder of what we were really there for, and we would then knuckle down cheerfully to the evening's task of making detailed plans and preparations for big events in the island's farming and social calendar: the spring ploughing match, the midsummer evening sheep-shearing competition, the high summer fun day and evening ceilidh to follow known as the 'Colonsay Capers', and, in the autumn, by the Root and Grain Show which was followed by a hugely enjoyable dinner dance and, almost invariably, the hangover.

Colonsay pier and harbour. The boathouse, bottom left, was my pottery, and the ferry lying alongside the busy pier is the Columba.

The pottery in the foreground, Glen Cottage to the rear.

Our home, Glen Cottage.

The potter at work.

Jane and Katie 'Photter'.

Our next-door neighbours: from left, Foelallie, Finlay, a bashful George and Catriona.

Brothers Neil and Ross Darroch returning from a fishing trip.

Three men and a boat: from left, Johnny Nicolson, 'Old Peter' MacAllister and Neil Darroch.

The Assistant Piermaster, aka 'the Potter'.

In the 'Cul-ree', Glen Cottage in the background. From right to left, 'Wee Roger' McIntyre, Finlay MacFadyen, 'Big Peter' MacAllister and visiting GPO man (?).

Boys' (and girls') ploys: Danny and Katie in the garden of Glen Cottage, and the Potter back from a successful trip to the lobster holes.

Danny Photter, Katie Photter and Georgie Photter.

'D.A.'/Donald Garvard and his brother-in-law, 'A.S.'/Andrew McNeill, waiting to pipe before Kate Strathcona's wedding.

Para Mor at the helm.

Ross Darroch and 'Jum' at the peats.

Angus Clark 'at the puffer' (coal boat).

What makes a community tick over happily most of the time? Is it more than a willing tolerance of each other's company, notwithstanding the human quirks, differences, things that one doesn't much like in oneself but finds harder to overlook in others – especially at the end of a long, hard or even unexceptional winter, when sunshine and new faces from the mainland have been in short supply and that scratchy, easily irritated feeling, known locally as 'barbed wire disease', is affecting the local populace, including yourself, like a flu that you just can't shake off?

Is it the seemingly mundane, day in day out, spontaneous good neighbourliness that shows itself in small acts of kindness, doing favours, sharing conversation, thoughts, concerns, laughter, work, play, the time of day? How necessary for community well-being are the pre-planned events in the calendar, like concerts and ceilidhs when locals and visitors alike come together to share and enjoy organised entertainment? How important is it for a community to have a good feeling about itself by working together to meet the lesser and greater challenges to its preferred way of life, rather than just feeling wearied and downhearted by the effort involved in what, at times, may seem like a never-ending struggle on too many fronts, after you have completed, or felt obliged to put aside, your day job or preferred alternatives?

As my involvement and interest in the life of the community grew, so the fairytale naivety of first impressions was replaced by a more realistic, though never entirely unromantic, appreciation of what made Colonsay tick and which aspects did most for me. It was, without a doubt, an affectionate and caring community, where family life and interconnections were strong and incomers, whether settlers or visitors, were often a little startled at first but soon captivated by the natural friendliness and generosity of the customary Hebridean welcome. Doors to island homes were not only never locked, they were, metaphorically at least, ever open, and even the briefest intended visit would almost invariably occasion a gentle but firm invocation from the lady of the house to sit yourself down and take a cup of tea, which would inevitably be accompanied by a 'piece' – not untypically a biscuit and cheese, a home-baked drop scone and jam, a slice of clootie dumpling perhaps, which would contain enough calories on its own to keep an active manual labourer ticking over happily for several days. Should you, for some reason or other which seemed perfectly valid to you at the time, attempt to decline the offer, albeit in the most mannerly and grateful way you could muster, the look of disappointment if not minor outrage on the face of those whose lintel you had crossed was usually such as to make you quickly change your mind, and settle down for a companionable 'blether' from which you would eventually move on feeling nourished in spirit and a pound or two heavier in body than when you arrived.

The islanders were particularly fond of children and tended to lavish unfeigned affection on them whenever an opportunity arose; and a new-born arrival in the community would bring coos of delight and presents in equal measure, including the occasional silver sixpence placed in the palm of the infant by older neighbours. The community's older members were visited and cared for by their families and neighbours, and generally took as full and equal a part in its shared life as they felt able or inclined to do. When someone died, just about every single able-bodied adult islander would turn out to remember them and their families at both church and graveside. On those rare but particularly difficult occasions when one of the island's young people had to be laid to rest, the feeling of shared hurt was very strong indeed, and seemed to draw on a very deep sense of communal togetherness.

It was a community with a wicked but affectionate sense of humour, which simply relished a good story, to be re-told and re-savoured time and time again as and when an opportune moment presented itself. A good story would build slowly and climax suddenly with a trenchant and epigrammatic punchline, such as 'he said possession was nine-tenths of the law, so I just showed him the tenth point and flung him out!' and they took particular delight in stories which showed the foibles of much-loved island characters. 'If I was to say I had leprosy, she'd be sure to say she had something worse!' as one fine old lady on the island once remarked, with some feeling, of her slightly younger and no less lovable sister: a story which encapsulated their respective characters and brought knowing pleasure to everyone in the community who heard it – and then sent it winging on its way round the island, on the unwritten but universally accepted grounds that if you came across a good story, you were duty-bound to share it asap.

The practical joke was a particular favourite of the boys next door – Dondie, the eldest, then Donald, Johnny and 'Wee Finlay' MacFadyen. April Fools Day gave them all the license they needed to take advantage of the unsuspecting, even those who knew them only too well. The supreme exponent was Donald, who took the opportunity offered to make a phone call to his uncle, Big Angus, who ran the shop and post office. Donald was a consummate impersonator, and had no difficulty whatsoever in persuading his uncle that the person at the end of the line was a rather shrill, well-bred and clearly eccentric Englishman, who was coming to the island on holiday for the very first time and was set on making quite sure that he would be able to have all the provisions he required ready and waiting for him on arrival. 'You'll get all you want here,' advised Big Angus confidently, but the gentleman still insisted on placing a long and exacting order which included things like tins of anchovies, which Angus was compelled to admit that he didn't currently have in stock. Ever the true gentleman himself, Angus tried not to show his increasing exasperation as the man at the end of the phone asked question after probing question about the shopping list that Angus was patiently compiling on his interrogator's behalf, but, eventually, he was able to hang up and turn to his by now rather concerned wife, Ella, with a gasket-blowing '*A Dhia nan Gras* [O God of the Graces], I don't know who that fellow was but, by heavens, he's got a screw loose!' Donald wasn't quite finished though, and wasted no time in getting himself and at least one of his brothers over to his relations, purportedly on just another, quite innocent social call, but in reality to savour the reaction as he revealed the awful truth to his father's well-fooled younger brother.

More typically, Colonsay humour was suffused with irony, ranging from the distinctly scathing variety, as in derogatory comments about the weather, to the gentler kind which allowed the islanders to rehearse their preferred take on the quirks and foibles of the human condition. Whenever there was a howling, screaming gale blowing the tops off the waves into white, smoking swirls, then the traditional comment, usually preceded by a dismissive sniff, was '*brios maith seolaidh*', 'a good sailing breeze'. Another favourite of Big Peter's was 'it's chilly for June', a greeting he would happily impart at any time of year, except June, and as and when air temperatures failed to match general expectations. Finlay's standby, delivered whenever the descending rain was particularly heavy and persistent, and each and every single time with the same air of long-suffering contempt, was 'It's a drowning match'. Light to moderate rain, however, he would refer to as 'it's just dry rain', a comment allegedly made by the island's laird to encourage some of his employees to get out of the van in which they had taken cover, and get on with the job in hand. It was an exhortation which Finlay had taken to heart, though not in quite the same way. Big Peter's pithy ironies weren't restricted to the weather: another favourite of his was 'success to temperance', a cheerily-delivered toast that almost invariably preceded his first sip of the day as he raised a pint of light ale to his bewhiskered lips, his refusal to accept a refill before going home often explained by '*Cha gabh* [I won't have one]: I've had an elegant sufficiency.'

No venue was better than the Hotel bar for some ironic storytelling, particularly a drinking story such as the often shared example about old Coll, Aldy's father, a famous character of yesteryear. Coll, road-mending outside the Hotel late one hot summer morning, was asked by an island visitor, who knew him well, if he would care to pop into the bar for a refreshment. 'No, thank you,' replied Coll, 'I never drink before lunchtime – forbye, I've had two already!' Wit was highly prized, and Colonsay had a Hebridean champion in island farmer Angus Clark, whose slow drawl was but a masterly camouflage for a very lively and humorous mind. We were walking off the pier together one day after the ferry had departed, and exchanged greetings with Dougie McGilvray, who was heading the other way to collect a parcel. For some reason Dougie wasn't wearing his dentures that morning, and I commented to Angus that Dougie looked slightly scary without his teeth in. 'Aye, right enough,' replied the deadpan Angus, 'but his bark will be worse than his bite,' the slow, fruity Hebridean inflections given to the key words only enhancing the impact of his latest witticism.

Self-sufficiency was much in evidence too, though, and those who had the quality in abundance generally seemed happy to share it with those who had a great deal less. None was ever more generous than our next door neighbour, Finlay, who distributed his surplus liberally to all those who came knocking at his door or, more specifically, looked for him in his corrugated-iron garage next door to Hazel Cottage. It was a veritable Aladdin's Cave, its walls and workbenches covered in a rich and varied vocabulary of different tools and gadgets, which he drew skilfully upon to resurrect the succession of sick vehicles that, along with their long-winded tales of woe, were presented to him on a regular basis by their grieving owners. As his closest neighbour and by far the least mechanically-minded male on the island, I must have brought and caused Finlay more grief than anyone he had ever come across before, but I never received anything less than a warm welcome, a hands-on (his) solution to the problem, more sympathy than I ever deserved and, without fail, tea as well, plus stories and laughter by the living-room fire (if it was evening) or the kitchen Rayburn (during the day) to round matters off properly.

Island life was not all rose-tinted, however. Islanders are no more immune than their mainland counterparts to the age-old pressures of trying to make ends meet, and otherwise doing okay by themselves and their families in life's varying circumstances. There were other realities too, deriving from an all too human self-insufficiency to meet some of the inevitable stresses and strains encountered living the remote rural life.

'Archers' syndrome' commonly affects small and isolated rural communities whose cast members all play parts, whether they want to or not, in everyday stories of country folk, in which both newsworthy and more trivial events in their notionally private lives are inevitably more closely observed by their fellow cast members than those observed would like, and which often end up being broadcast, occasionally with a storyteller's embellishment or two, to a wider local audience. The familiar goldfish bowl, which seems so friendly and comforting most of the time, can suddenly feel suffocatingly small, even when no-one else but oneself might actually be responsible for the negative thought which disturbed one's usual level of equilibrium.

Creeping peer pressure could come out of a clear blue sky, like the one I bent my back under one sunny April morning as I started to plant out my seed potatoes in the corner of our small garden plot, located right next to the busiest section of the island's 'main' road. It was just too handy and irresistible for passers-by to stop. No sooner had old Ross climbed back onto his bike after pointing out that one-time Glen Cottage resident, 'Alec the Post', never planted his tatties before May Day with a conclusive 'Aye, and Alec always had great potatoes', than Ross's brother, Neil, had leant his bike against the fence and was scratching the back of his head and speculating that I might have been better to plant the drills east to west rather than north to south. Aldy, Jasper and Big Peter all drew purposefully to a halt too, and left me with further questions, not just about unfortunate deficiencies in both my plot preparation and choice of potato variety, but ultimately, it began to feel, myself. When Ian 'Seaview' rounded off the session by pulling up in his yellow Ford Capri, winding down the window and telling me that 'They'll not come to much there, Potter' before giving me a chance to defend myself and roaring off on his latest mission, I decided to go inside, lick my wounds and finish off my gardening by twilight. I needn't have worried though: the new potatoes grew just fine.

The apparent freedom offered by island life could prove hard to handle for even those born to it, let alone those who were discovering it. Most islanders had a rare degree of control over how they spent their time: they were not constrained by commuter timetables or ever-present employers watching their every move; they were, by and large, their own bosses, doing what needed to be done but with an enviable amount of time to spare, and no streetloads of neighbouring Joneses by whom to feel reproached in a community where a relaxed and egalitarian approach to life was considered the socially acceptable norm.

Some, like the potter, regularly over-indulged the licence to choose the softer option rather than applying the time and effort required by the workplace. Time there was, too, for the seductive diversion of pub-assisted conviviality, which was great fun at times but with more than one price to pay. A few fine people paid too heavily when the drink got the better of them and, although the community showed them great tolerance and understanding, it discomfited even the most understanding of native islanders when they witnessed one of their own succumbing to the self-destructive effects of alcohol addiction. Taking the occasional 'spree', as it was euphemistically called, was looked upon almost affectionately – particularly when the sprees generated, as they usually did, a humorous anecdote or two. But a big spree, a serious spree, was altogether more difficult for everyone else to ignore, when it resulted in some well-loved member of the community going off on a depressing bender lasting days on end. Turning a blind eye might not be enough to stop yourself feeling like a collaborator as you silently witnessed a 'spree-wagon', typically a battered landrover or a tractor and trailer, with its complement of 'spree-merchants' – such sprees had their own descriptive vocabulary – wending its unmistakeable way to or from the pub.

How then to square the use and the effects of the demonising drink with the deep, though often well-lubricated, sense of pleasure and affection for the community that would be derived, for example, from attending a good going Friday or Saturday evening ceilidh in the village hall at Kiloran in the centre of the island? As vivid illustrations of all that seemed good about Colonsay's community life, they could not be bettered. Most islanders would look forward to these events, which though they had long intervals in between during the winter months, became fortnightly to weekly, or even two or three times weekly, during the busiest months of the summer holiday season, when the island population was swelled by its 'visitors', the temporarily resident holidaymakers. Virtually the whole island would attend them too; parents with tiny tots and bigger children arriving around eight o'clock to join the older folk, who also liked to get there promptly; but with the numbers ever-increasing as the evening wore on and they were joined by the younger ones, who had stopped by the pub first for a refreshment to quicken their appetite for the evening's entertainment.

The children would be itching for the evening to get going and, not before time as far as they were concerned, Dougie McGilvray would take up his traditional position at the back right-hand corner of the stage overlooking the dance floor and put the record on the gramophone for the first of the evening's Scottish country dances, a St Bernard's Waltz, which at least stirred the memory, if not initially reluctant joints; to be followed in due course by the full menu of energetic Strip the Willows, Boston Two-Steps, Dashing White Sergeants, Eightsome Reels, Gay Gordons, Highland Schottisches, Military Two-Steps, Waltz Country Dances and the like, interspersed with a St Bernard's Waltz or two to let people to get their breath back. Such were the staple fare of those Colonsay ceilidhs.

If there were live artists, as there often were, to play their versions of the familiar tunes, then Dougie would be released from his duties: if not, then he attended to them diligently, sustained by a succession of cups of tea, sandwiches and endless roll-ups, and if the record seemed only to get stuck when he had just nipped round the back for the quickest of comfort breaks, then his return to the stage just added to the general enjoyment of the occasion. He sat and watched from his eyrie as all human life of the Colonsay ceilidh variety passed below him on the slip-perined dance floor: the tiniest of tots doing their own creative thing, slightly bigger children dancing with parents, grandpar-ents and each other; old hands who had discovered they were nineteen again and danced with as much relish but much better technique than those who really were; while the young crowd fresh from the pub threw themselves into the dances with spar-kling-eyed abandon and wheechs of delight. The dance floor did its best to support and encourage the dancers by taking on the guise of a wooden trampoline, and viewed from a distance the glowing and pulsating village hall could have been mistaken for an intergalactic spacecraft preparing itself for imminent blast-off.

Halfway through the evening a halt would be brought to the proceedings to allow tea, sandwiches and home-baking, donated and served up by the ladies of the island, but with a couple of willing males put in charge of the giant aluminium teapots for refills, all gratefully taken on board by those present while waiting for the all-important raffle to be drawn. If some were temporarily absent during the break, it was only because they were faithfully observing both the island custom and the then licensing laws by sitting in cars having a companionable and vaguely surreptitious dram, though it was surely not just the alcohol that left you with the intoxicating sense of time having slowed to a dreamlike standstill, seemingly to allow each ceili-dhing participant to live the moment they were sharing as fully as they were able and, so it seemed, to feel the beating heart of this magic-making island.

Never was that sense of fellow-feeling more tangible than at a Colonsay New Year, when the same mix of drams, cups of tea, comestible ballast, stories, music, fun, laughter and general goodwill would flow in copious measure from Hogmanay till around the third of January, when supplies and stamina eventu-ally petered out.

Informal and spontaneous as it was, the occasion was bound by the tradition of 'first footing', which involved visiting as many islanders as possible in the first hours and days after the clock had struck midnight to mark the dying moments of the passing year and the fresh appearance of the new one. In 1970s Colonsay, first-footing took two forms, the traditional, and something more akin to a Mexican wave.

The time-honoured approach was to visit each of your immediate neighbours' houses in turn and with a kiss and a hug or a shake of the hand to wish everyone present a 'Happy/ Good New Year', in Gaelic, *Bliadhna mhaith ur,* or in English, to which the traditional Gaelic response was *Mar sin dhuit fhein agus moran dhuibhe,* 'and the same to you and many of them'. The host would pour you a dram, and you would raise your glasses and wish each other and everyone else present a happy new year again. Sightings of favourite island characters and news of the night's escapades thus far would be exchanged, and soon the stories would start with that most familiar entrée, '*Tha cuin agam . . .*', 'I remember . . .', only to be interrupted by the hostess pressing tea, sandwiches and home-baking on to you, or by the arrival of other first-footers, or someone being moved or encouraged to sing a song and/or play a tune on the fiddle, the box (accordion) or guitar. You would never leave the house without reciprocating the offer of a dram and, as can be deduced, the rate of progress from house to house was likely to be slow and get slower as the night and the effects of the Hebridean hospitality wore on. It was very good fun though.

The Mexican wave approach was practiced by the younger and more fancy-free members of the community, who had developed their own complementary tradition of doing a collective circuit of the island, calling in en masse on every house that had left a welcoming light on – and even, occasionally, some who had made the fatal mistake of pointedly turning out the lights and going to bed before they had called, a social gaffe that would almost certainly bring out the *bandido* in the leaders of this gang of cheerful revellers, even though if you lived near the end of the circuit, in Glen Cottage for example, you might not receive your invasion till nearly breakfast time when the wide-eyed children of the house would pick their way, agog, through the mass of limbs and bottles that now filled the floor of their living room, on the lookout for a parent or two and nothing stronger than warm milk and Weetabix.

By the afternoon of the first of January many islanders, a few temporarily spent *bandidos* excepted, were on the move again, first-footing those they had missed the night before, but now rather more on the basis of congenial rehydration by tea than dehydration from further modicums of alcohol. Come the evening there would be a New Year dance and ceilidh in the village hall, bringing with it the usual feelings of island togetherness and good cheer. Then home to blessed bed or, much more likely, not – as further visitors usually arrived, typically soloists who liked nothing better than night-long one-to-one conversations about the meaning of life, which soon tended to take on a confusingly dreamlike quality.

As a result you might well find yourself seeing the reluctant rising of the second consecutive dawn of the New Year over an island which, though showing some signs of weakening, was still up for just a little bit more conviviality, even though parts of it were already trying to return to normality. On the evening of the second the younger troops would muster together once more in Jessie's ever-accommodating home from home, where two of the island's favourite sons, Niall Brown and 'Peedie' McNeill, both studying in Edinburgh to be teachers, would sing songs and make wonderful music together on their guitars, while the rest sang along, nodded off, came to, interrupted, compared New Year tales of derring-do and didn't, joked, laughed, fortified themselves on Jessie's unstinting offerings of soup, sandwiches, rabbit stew, cake and tea, possibly plus a reviver or two, and generally enjoyed the longest and most enjoyable house-ceilidh in the island calendar.

It was that same evening of the year that Big Peter and I received – or was it took – official licence from our respective spouses to head off together in his ex-post office van to first-foot some of the older members of the community. First stop was outside the now dark and spookily silent village hall, opposite two semidetached cottages. In the first, immaculately kept jewel of an island home lived *Ruaridh Caol*, 'thin Roger', and 'Old Mary' McIntyre, his gentle and lovely wife. In the second, sitting well to the side of an invariably roaring open fire with the orange reflections of the flames dancing on the opposite wall, the equally welcoming *Donnachadh Alastair Og*, 'Duncan, son of young Alasdair', McNeill, better known as 'Duncan Balnahard' after the farm in the north of the island that he had worked on for so many years.

Hours and hours of reminiscing in Gaelic would pass between Peter and all our respective hosts that night, the potter's hardly difficult role being to provide an appreciative and spellbound audience, and wonder how it was that he seemed to understand so much more of the language of the Garden of Eden than he ever did when sober. After another short stop of an hour or so in Hugh and Betty Galbraith's house, also in Kiloran, we would head on to Kilchattan wondering, unnecessarily as it invariably turned out, whether at about three in the morning there would still be a light on at *Seaview*, the crofthouse of old Dugie McKinnon, originally from Mull, his brother 'Squeaky' and their son Ian, always referred to simply as 'Seaview' and who would have been long since ensconced at Jessie Machrin's house. The two brothers, like their neighbours down the hill at *Homefield*, brother and sister Neil and Mary Martin, born in the last decades of the nineteenth century and survivors from a time when the population of the island was three times as great and every croft was worked to its utmost to sustain large families, were always delighted to receive a visit from Para Mor, whether he was calling on business to fix a fault with their phoneline or for any other occasion. Big Peter was a fund of intelligence to be sure, but more an inexhaustible repository of stories about islanders and island life; well-honed, tellingly observed, humourful, often outrageously, wickedly funny stories that could leave his audience of any age gasping at his cheek, crying with laughter and eager for more. He was never on more sparkling form than at New Year, which is why lights stayed on and one member of his island-wide fan club was only too happy to act as chauffeur.

Our final port of call, at an hour when more health-conscious people have achieved most of their beauty sleep, was Machrins, where there was little sign that Jessie would ever get her house back. Hughie McConnell, who with his Zapata moustache and bedroom eyes was the very embodiment of a Hebridean *bandido*, would happily perform his annual re-enactment of 'the drunken piper' routine, others would be badgered till they had aired their party pieces, and Neil and Pedie would go on singing like linties till conversation eventually slowed, like time itself, to a trickle. In the end, this longest and friendliest of nights gave way to a suddenly bleary-eyed dawning of the third day of another Colonsay New Year; and the piermaster would turn to his assistant and say to him in Gaelic, *'S'e an t'am air son folbh dhachaidh, a Photter'*, 'It's the time for going home, o Potter'. And so, companionably, we did.

9

MAKING SERIOUS FUN

A stream of playfulness bubbled away blithely through Colon-say's way of life, and though most of its self-expression was spontaneous, a serious amount of organisational effort went into in making sure that 'Are you coming out to play?' opportunities weren't just confined to the island's children. For a tiny community of a little over a hundred souls, there really were an awful lot of organised events, albeit with much fun to be had as well as money to be generated for good causes. But if all the voluntary man and woman hours involved in their planning, preparation and running – particularly over the summer months – were added up and divided by the number of able-bodied adults in the island, then the investment of community effort was impressive. The island, though, didn't really give this aspect a second thought: it was part of the natural order of things and taken much for granted.

None of the resulting happenings was more welcoming and enjoyable than a ceilidh dance or a concert in the village hall, each the result of hours of unsung, behind-the-scenes graft by members of one or other of the community groups, like the Village Hall committee, the Gun Club or the WRI. Almost all were fundraisers too, and badged accordingly, like 'The Shipwrecked Mariners Ceilidh' which described the fundraising cause and not the late arrivals from the pub. This ceilidh, my diary remembers, was the third one, in addition to another concert, that was laid on in the Village Hall in the space of eight August days in 1978.

No local group was more active over the year than the Colonsay Young Farmers Club and, as its unexpectedly appointed Secretary, I soon learnt just how much attention to brain-curdling detail, let alone time and sometimes frenetic activity, club members had to commit in putting on events like the Colonsay Capers, a Saturday afternoon in August of pure fun dreamt up by Donald MacFadyen, the third of our neighbours' teenage sons, whose mind was alive with humour. The programme featured welly-throwing, jelly-eating and slippery trailer 'ocean-emptying' competitions amongst many others, and culminated with a six-a-side tug of war between mixed teams of adults and children. It too was followed by a dance in the Village Hall. The autumn Root and Grain Show was a two-day affair, starting on the Thursday with a dinner dance in the Hotel, a day off to recover and then the Show itself on the Saturday afternoon, to be cleared away and followed by another ceilidh dance, which featured a fancy dress show for all ages. At least the locals didn't have the added anxiety of having to judge any of the Show's exhibits – an awesome responsibility which the mainland invitees were always left to shoulder, leaving local reputations intact.

Where, in ordinary daily life, a naked display of the competitive instinct would have elicited a communal 'tut-tut', in the context of an island-wide challenge to produce a champion onion set or a best Victoria spongecake, then it was quite okay to let it show. Thus, grown men whose waistlines now matched their seniority, could be seen at the annual Sports Day, held in high summer in a walled field near Machrins known as the *'phairc ur'*, 'the new field', taking devil-may-care risks with their health as they over-exerted themselves in the traditional mix of track and field events, even though they knew it was all for little or nothing. An evergreen Archie McConnell always seemed to win everything, as he had been doing for years and years. Even worse, some of the selfsame culprits might be involved later on in the year making unsupported allegations about the origins of the prize-winning onions which, they concurred, had been of suspiciously shop-bought perfection.

Though the various Ladies Races on Sports Day proved that it wasn't only the island men who loved to compete, organised competitions were, by and large, showpieces for the male of that still chauvinistic era. Whether with football, shotgun, dart, plough or sheep shears, such events were mainly just extra ploys for the island boys, who counted crofters, farmers, postmen, piermen and potters amongst the ever-faithful. Though I never did more than spectate admiringly at the spring ploughing match and ponder the slow build-up of unfurling furrows, I was given stopwatch responsibility at the sheep-shearing competition at Scalasaig Farm, where turnaround speed was of the essence, provided the creature being shorn did not end up looking like a war victim: in which case, swabs were applied and points deducted.

Sunday afternoon football games during the summer months were mostly end to end free-for-alls, full of sound and fury signifying nothing, all of which I found very therapeutic and exhausting. The main skill involved was avoiding the ankle-turning rabbit scrapes, something which the locals understood better than the visitors. Darts matches were convivial affairs and dark horses like Jasper Brown, who had only one good eye, would become ever more likely to win as the evenings wore on to their often ridiculously late-night finales. Clay-pigeon shooting matches, held on the greensward next to the clean white sands and clear blue seas of Machrins Bay, were more seriously competitive and drew in devotees young, old and in between, including some of the island's most senior stalwarts like old Ross who could still shoot like Buffalo Bill. My personal ambition was to try to beat my neighbour Finlay's brother, 'Big Angus' MaFadyen, local postman and crackshot, who had patiently taught me how to handle a shotgun properly, as he would cheerfully remind me if I ever managed to pip him by a point or, more usually, when I didn't.

Humour, Colonsay's golden thread, flowed through all these sporting occasions, but there was one competition to come or, more accurately, come again, and which, for a sporting challenge combined with unbeatable 'craic', surpassed them all. In the late summer of 1978 a red-bearded Irishman, his wife and small children, appeared as seemingly out of nowhere as the family in

Glen Cottage had done six years previously and came to live on the island. Kevin and Christa Byrne had bought the Colonsay Hotel, and it soon became clear that Kevin was a man simply bursting with ideas which he would share enthusiastically with his regular callers at the bar. For most islanders, including those who had gone native, there was little wrong with setting a hare running for the purpose of making good conversation, although the customary response was to point out the potential pitfalls in ever acting on such flights of fancy, even though one could never quite rule out the possibility altogether. In the meantime, no good would be likely to come from rushing headlong into precipitate action – a well-trusted precautionary principle of island life that was traditionally conveyed with a sniff and a slow and pitying shake of the head.

Imagine, then, the deep intake of Inner Hebridean breath that occurred when the new hotelier had the temerity to take an action which exploded the 'Ach, well, *cha n'eil fhios agamsa*,' 'I don't know' view on the island's long-abandoned golf course and about which familiar tales and doubts were shared whenever anyone wondered whether it might ever be possible to get it going again. Almost overnight, it seemed, Kevin had rooted out a long lost map of the course, found eighteen old oil drums of the smaller variety, painted them green, scrawled big white numbers on them, implanted them in the general vicinity of where the eighteen tees used to be, re-staked a claim on the postage stamp-sized areas of unimproved turf that had once formed the greens by digging eighteen holes and sticking fluttering flags in them and, without any further ceremony, declared the Colonsay Golf Course, which had fallen into disuse over twenty years previously and melted back without trace into the soft, green machair land, open once more for sporting business.

The previous doubters, myself included, exhaled slowly and looked at each other. Shock and suspicion were overtaken by curiosity, which quickly transformed into lively interest. Big Peter made a rare pilgrimage to his loft and extricated his father's long-abandoned golf clubs, others acquired sets of smart second-hand ones from mainland sources. My father-in-law kindly gave me his first set of pre-war golf clubs which looked like props from a Bertie Wooster story, and comprised hickory-shafted drivers and irons with names like brassies and mashie-niblicks, and came in their original canvas and leather golf bag. They still did the business though.

No matter that very few locals had ever tried to play golf before; the prospect of sampling this new and unexpected ploy was irresistible and very soon a surprisingly large cross-section of Colonsay society – men, women and youngsters – were giving it a whirl, as would many delighted visitors. To describe the newly resurrected golf course as challenging is as inadequate as saying it was beautiful: it was and remains a world-beating cracker on both counts. The vista from the then first tee was inspirational: laid out to the west like a giant's picnic blanket, the great swathe of green and gently undulating machair land that carries the golf course and its unsuspecting golfers on their unforgettable coastal journey. The sights and the sounds of the sea, the views of the meandering shoreline, the striking headlands and the restless Atlantic Ocean beyond are to die for, whenever your golfing head was not down.

It would not always be up, that was certain, for this course was a wolf in sheep's clothing, an authentic reincarnation of those medieval duneland originals from which the modern version of the game of golf, played on today's improbably manicured courses, has since evolved. This reawakened Kraken was designed by and subject to the forces of Mother Nature and, save for Kevin's lightest of touches, the human hand was nowhere to be seen in its re-creation. Fairways were no more than generalisations to describe the unimproved intervals between tee and green, though the random pockmarking of rabbit scrapes and holes waiting to gobble up your drive could hardly be described as fair. The greens were delineated by an occasional mowing of the natural machairland turf, and with not much to choose between what had and hadn't felt the attention of the blade. In any event, the state of the waiting greens was always variable, depending, as it were, on the recent movements of animals. Rabbit and sheep droppings could be easily enough dealt with by using the putter to clear a path for the ball to the hole, but the freshly laid cowpat was another matter, particularly when you discovered that it had, with a shloop and a splatter, swallowed your pitch shot.

These weren't the only natural hazards, some more exasperating than others, that were capable of reducing grown men to tears of frustration or sometimes helpless merriment. It was bad enough to see, or occasionally hear, your drive ricocheting, usually into oblivion but occasionally right back over your head, off one of the outcrops of bare rock that stand sentinel to some of the holes. Worse, far worse, is to watch your unexpectedly well struck ball heading, for a rarity, straight as a die towards its intended destination, only for it to be picked up by a raven and proudly carried away to its nest to impress its partner or simply to add to its collection, the cries of outrage coming from the dispossessed golfer all but drowned out by the ironic cheers and belly laughter coming from one's golfing partners.

This was a singularly undomesticated links course, with, to be sure, rocks, rabbit holes, ravens, rougher than rough rough of the most impenetrable sedge and meanest marram grass; but it was also, without a doubt, one with a sweet and beckoning side, brimful of Hebridean charm and grace notes. Where else can you tee off from the top of an Iron Age fortlet, aptly called *Dunan gath gaoith,* 'Fortlet of the stinging wind', which you hoped was at your back when you launched an ever-hopeful drive towards the minute green guarded by a burn, a road and a stone dyke? What could beat the stunning seascape setting of the course's most challenging section, the journey past the raised beaches and around the dramatic headland of *Dun Ghallain,* an Iron Age chieftain's long-abandoned fort, whose rocky stronghold still guards the entrance to the long, sandy bay of *Port Lobh,* 'smelly seaweed port', and looks out onto the reefs and skerries of nearby Ardskenish? What could possibly spoil a good walk round the machair on a Saturday or Sunday afternoon, with the scent of wild flowers in the air and skylarks singing their hearts out high overhead? Other, that is, than a disastrous round of golf.

On such blessed days it shouldn't have mattered when my hickory-shafted driver demonstrated yet again that it had a mind of its own and a banana-shaped follow-through to match, spraying lustily hit drives in wild and entirely random parabolas. I was just happy to be there, in the very best of local company, as we began to hack our way round the machair in scores which started off around 130+ but gradually came down and down, until we each broke the one hundred barrier and felt as if the purpose of our lives had finally been fulfilled.

It was sublime and surreal escapism that suited the island character to a rediscovered tee, an exercise of much futility, save for the fact that fun and humour flowed. What else would have tempted Angus Clark, Davie McConnell and me to deliberately test ourselves against a force-9 gale howling in off the Atlantic, dressed in oilskins and wellies? We, who had been born just too late for National Service, would at last face up to a real challenge, and it wasn't easy. Making headway around Dun Ghallain in the teeth of the gale was all but impossible, but Davie, in particular, showed a defiance against all the odds that would have served his country well. Even he though finally succumbed at the uphill seventeenth (these days the eighteenth) – a devil in waiting even on a good day – where his score matched the hole and, during the compilation of which, he was moved to deliver a memorable if unprintable soliloquy which summed up those wretched moments of mental turmoil and torture that all who try to play the game of golf must sooner or later experience. It was addressed to his ball which, not for the first time, had gone awol. In the space of three adjectives and a noun he venomously disparaged its size, its colour (though never in a racist way) and its morals, which he clearly connected with its loose-living forebears. He also made it clear beyond any possible doubt that should he ever come across it again he would take very considerable personal satisfaction in murdering it. Angus and I believed him completely, and were relieved that the ball had the good sense to stay hidden.

But the hardest fun-making challenge I ever had to respond to was to take my turn, as all the Young Farmers Club members had to in due course, at the top table at the annual Root and Grain Show dinner and deliver one of the expected speeches. I suggested Davie could take my place, but our esteemed president, Ian 'Seaview' MacKinnon, would have none of it. This would be a first for me and I went into a prolonged panic. After much agonising and pacing up and down the pottery with the door closed, I ground out the following which served its purpose on the night and paved the way for other equally despairing efforts in later years.

THE SAD STORY OF A YOUNG FARMER
WHO LEFT IT TOO LATE

I am a young farmer and I live on the croft,
Though my head it is hard, my heart it is soft.
I've a second-hand tractor, ten sheep and a cow,
And I know what I want, but the question is how?
How does a young fellow in the prime of his life
Go about finding the like of a wife?
I don't know what it is that is wrong with this glen –
Either not enough women or too many men.
There was Morag McKinley – I liked her just fine –
But she married Finlay who's no friend of mine!
There is Flora McTaggart, old Angus's daughter
And though I am short she is very much shorter.
She stands three-foot-six and weighs nineteen stone
And I just couldn't manage her all on my own.
And Effie MacDonald who works at the shop,
Once she starts talking forgets when to stop.
I tried advertising but the only reply
Was from my cousin Archie who thinks he is fly.
He pretended his name was Lizzie MacRae,
Who would give me a trial for a year and a day.
She said she loved working and wouldn't complain

If she was out on the croft and it started to rain –
It was the photo she sent that aroused my suspicion
Which was obviously taken without her permission!
I found it exciting and was feeling quite frisky
When I realised the envelope smelt of old whisky.
Next time I saw Archie he laughed like a drain,
But he won't be deceiving me like that again.
And now I'm gone thirty, soon forty I'll be,
And all those young ladies they don't think of me.
What on earth will I do if I don't find a wife –
I can't be a young farmer the rest of my life?
So, young, young farmer your duty you see
Is get married quickly or you'll end up like me!

10
Feu!

The resident islanders were bound together by an intimate and essentially egalitarian way of life that flowed naturally from living in the same small, isolated community and sharing in its unique life story and round of daily happenings. Almost every aspect of this seemed to stem from its attractively different culture and to reflect the deeply embedded beliefs and habits of the native Gaels whose underlying generosity of spirit, deeply tolerant understanding of human nature, inexhaustible love of companionable and humour-laced conversation, in whichever language it was expressed, made getting to know the island so rewarding.

Colonsay life was also characterised, however, by a close but ambivalent relationship with the 'Estate', as it was commonly referred to, which in the early 1970s still owned almost every single one of Colonsay and Oronsay's 11,000-odd acres, including every farm and croft and every steading and house built on them. With the sole exceptions of the Church of Scotland minister, the Primary School head teacher and the doctor, everyone paid rent to the island proprietor and 'laird', Lord Strathcona and Mount Royal, for their security of tenure and their ultimate ability, therefore, to live and work there.

It was, strictly speaking, a feudal relationship: of legal obligations and business dealings, the one towards the other, that inevitably generated many 'them and us' moments. The stories arising would be told and re-told as the occasion might warrant but, despite their inevitable moments of humour, they usually seemed to reinforce feelings of negativity and resignation that

Colonsay would remain for ever in non-egalitarian thrall to lairds who were inclined, it so easily seemed, to put their own interests before island ones; even if such a one-sided portrayal did not always stand up to impartial analysis.

As a new but loyal member of the 'us' team, pre-programmed by my bolshevik upbringing to be suspicious of all 'them' teams, I entertained few doubts about where my own prejudices lay. Although, in common with others, I felt rather depressed and disempowered by this feudal reality, I always got on, as did everyone else, with the large and outgoing Strathcona family during their regular stays on the island, when they would intermingle happily and noisily with the rest of the community.

My rapidly developing sense of scepticism over the power and influence of the Estate did not, however, make me any less curious or ploy-inclined when, only a couple of months after moving to the island, Aldy called into the pottery to ask if I could give him a lift to 'rent day' at the 'big house' in Kiloran. He unquestioningly assumed that like every other tenant I would not dream of missing this time-honoured event in the annual calendar. I, on the other hand, had failed to grasp its importance and was all set to casually give it a miss until Aldy put me right. He pointed out that, not only did it give every tenant an opportunity for a potentially useful private discussion with the island's landlord and his factor, or estate manager, about any tenancy issues, this tête-à-tête was always accompanied by the offer of a good dram, the age-old expression of Highland and Island hospitality. Aldy, who enjoyed a dram at least as much as any other islander, also testified that, where particularly tricky tenancy problems were being resolved, more than one dram might conceivably be offered.

Now better informed, I could see that it would be a waste of an opportunity to decline the invitation, and the following day a smartly suited Aldy and an habitually scruffier potter made their way in the Hillman across the island to the Estate Office, located in Colonsay House, the laird's impressive mansion, so picturesquely set, with its spacious gardens, in the lushly wooded heart of the island. As we rolled up like visiting tradesmen to the back-door termination of its long driveway, we bumped into other much tidier-looking than usual islanders who were just leaving or arriving to take their place in the queue. We sat ourselves down in the waiting area like schoolboys outside the Headmaster's office, listening to the muted mumble of voices within and waiting for the oak-panelled door to open so that we could try to gauge whether the previous interview had gone well and if the Laird and his factor would be feeling benign or irritated with their tenantry.

Aldy was first in, and re-emerged not long after with a wink and a discreetly raised forefinger to indicate that it had not been a two-dram meeting. My turn came next, and I was given a cordial welcome and a decent dram, which went straight to my head and left me a bit confused about what had really transpired, other than my handing over a rent in advance cheque for the six-month period between the 'term' dates of Martinmas and Whitsun, as my lease for Glen Cottage specified. Whether it was the effect of the alcohol taken in the afternoon or of the journey backwards in time, the experience was strangely disorienting, and I could not get rid of the feeling that the two gentlemen in the big house had been keeping more than just the chance of a refill to themselves.

That this rent-day event seemed to fall into abeyance so quickly after my first encounter with it surely had much more to do with the Strathconas' feeling about its relevance than any suspicions which they might reasonably have formed about the bolshevik they had, albeit for a mutually agreed return, come to realise they had invited to live on their estate.

For not many more term days passed before I decided to get bolshie about my rent level which, my regular visitors to the pottery had advised me to my red-faced frustration, was at least double what anyone else was paying for equivalent housing on the island that was in better condition. The trigger for rebellion was the Estate's proposal to increase island rents where lease conditions allowed, in my own case by 25%. The advisory letter from the Estate's factor caused something of a stir amongst my friends and neighbours and I boldly announced to them that I for one would strike a blow for the resistance by duly registering my protest with the Rent Officer, the Glasgow-based public official whose responsibility it was to mediate in such matters. Who else might be willing to join me, I wondered like the Little Red Hen, as we complained amongst ourselves about the imposition and bemoaned the cheek of the Estate for forcing the increase upon us?

At the end of the day it was just Big Peter and me who decided to write letters of objection to the Rent Officer who, a few weeks later came to visit us and, as a result, issued a notice almost halving my rent and reinstating Big Peter's former rent level. The Estate – i.e. Lord Strathcona on advice from his factor, or was it the other way round? – appealed the decision, which meant that a three-man Rent Assessment Committee was also obliged to take the ferry to Colonsay to inspect each property in the company of its tenant and the Estate factor and issue a final adjudication upon the matter. In my own case I gave them a guided tour of the self-evident defects in house condition, which unarguably rendered the property 'Below Tolerable Standard', and I drew their attention to the unfavourable rent comparisons. The factor made the case for the defence, but the tribunal found in my favour and reduced the rent even further than the Rent Officer, an outcome which, it soon became clear to me, had done nothing to raise the Estate's opinion of the potter who they had helped to get started in 'their' island.

Was the rent the Estate charged me really too high, or the rents it was charging everyone else simply too low? Was the 'extra' amount of money I was paying for the home in which I was discovering so much happiness and fulfilment really too much or too trifling to question? The issues I felt impelled to raise with the Estate came partly from the sense of frustration that my favourite islanders would on the one hand decry the alleged injustices perpetuated by their landlords, but invariably shake their heads knowingly when I suggested that some reasoned opposition might be justified. The answer to this conundrum was that during their lifetimes islanders had many occasions to reflect upon the very real power of a laird – any laird – with such extensive ownership control over the material conditions of their lives and such ability in consequence to frustrate their ambitions, later if not sooner. Safer, it seemed to the hardened local, to accept the inherent inequality in the relationship than to draw attention to oneself, and quite possibly make matters more problematic, if not now then in the longer term. This view was as arguably right, in the circumstances, as mine was wrong; for when, in due course, the seven-year lease of the boathouse I rented for my pottery came up for renewal, there was no Rent Officer's protection available for such business premises and my rent was doubled, take it or leave it. By that time I was already part-minded to move on, but this outcome seemed to confirm the widely-held view that a tenant would eventually reap what he sowed if he put his head above the parapet.

Another popular view was that estate factors were more to blame than the lairds for pushing rents up since, the theory went, their management fees were percentage-based and would increase proportionately. In any event, islanders generally had few deferential inhibitions about letting the factor know what they thought, whereas they were predisposed to show much greater affection, as well as deference, towards the man who, while still being the laird, was *their* laird, and who, at a more fundamental human level, was just another well-understood island character with whom they had long shared their island lives.

Factors were fairer game, though. They all seemed to originate from a world apart in far-removed parts of the mainland, before being despatched, suitably attired in corduroy trousers, tweed jackets, waxed waterproofs and flat caps, to carry out their business on the estates of the wilder and less orderly west coast. They knew that irritating Hebridean trials and tribulations would invariably be waiting there, to probe and test the limits of their skills and patience whenever they ventured onto Colonsay, notwithstanding the customary warmth and hospitality which the islanders accorded all visitors whether regular or occasional – and the traditional welcome did not exclude factors.

Nevertheless, few would have been well enough prepared for the directness of the 'no need to beat about the bush' greeting that Oronsay farmer, piper and Second World War soldier, Andrew ('A.S.') McNeill, gave to one relatively inexperienced, though perfectly dressed, factor as he strode confidently down the narrow roadway from the pier, having just disembarked from the ferry. Andrew, who was simultaneously heading towards the boat, took full advantage of this unexpected opportunity to buttonhole the man he believed was personally responsible for neglecting some important factorial responsibilities as far as the farm and farmhouse he paid the Estate rent for was concerned. Unimpressed by the noncommittal response he was receiving, the farmer took a step closer to his interviewee to add a little emphasis to the point he was making. Reacting instinctively, the factor jerked his head back, inadvertently loosening the grip on his smart tweed cap. A perfectly timed gust of wind did the rest and the now airborne bonnet flew over the safety railing like a well-launched frisbee and landed far below where the sea was surging vigorously against the legs of the pier and the older granite harbour to which it was attached.

This mishap brought the conversation to an end as suddenly as it had begun, and the parties went about their separate business. Andrew, feeling somewhat improved by the exchange, strode on to collect a parcel that had just come off the ferry, sharing the story with the piermaster and his assistant as he did so. The factor, looking less buoyant, went to hunt for his cap which, being fairly seaweed-coloured, proved hard to find. Later that day and from the cover of the pottery I caught sight of a solitary and bare-headed figure scouring the shore after the tide had gone out, before successfully recovering a now rather forlorn-looking piece of flotsam. If the factor's spirits had also been dampened by the experience, then the same could not be said for the Oronsay farmer who was inspired by the incident to compose a jaunty pipe tune that he called 'The Factor's Bunnet', and which soon attracted the critical acclaim of local audiences. They particularly admired the musical highlight of the piece, an exuberant and extended wheeech from the pipes that vividly conjures up the sight and sound of the dislodged cap as it made its short but dramatic maiden flight from its position of eminence to the watery depths below.

The personal relationship with the Estate, its factor and its lairds, was so well ingrained and understood that no islander was prepared for the shock that came just before Christmas 1974, when every householder on the island received a personal letter from Lord and Lady Strathcona saying that it had 'proved impossible to reconcile the demands of a working life in London, and those of a growing family, with living in Colonsay and giving proper care to the needs of the island', and that, with very great sadness, they had decided to put the island on the market the following May.

As an occasional rebel I felt the sale might present an opportunity for beneficial change, and when the local MP, a Scottish Nationalist, tabled a motion in the House of Commons demanding that the then Labour Government step in to buy both Colonsay and Oronsay, I day-dreamed as to whether such a big change might be possible. The majority of islanders, however, were clearly far less keen on any alteration to the status quo, though the popular view remained that the island had gone downhill since the 'Old Laird' had died in 1959 and his son, the new laird, had been forced to make big money-saving changes, axing all but a handful of the till then multitudinous Estate jobs. The resulting population loss had been described at the time in the popular press as 'another Highland clearance', but the age-old paternalism of the laird–islander relationship seemed to have survived this shock, its foundations intact. Most islanders still felt bound by the personal as well as practical ties they had with their laird, and he continued to exercise a degree of paternalistic influence over their lives, albeit in ways which he believed were in the island's, as well as his own, best interests.

The question as to whether Colonsay would be better off with new lairds rather than the old ones was given one answer the following spring when the island was taken off the market although Oronsay, which was sold a couple of years later to a distillery magnate, was kept on it. Lord Strathcona made the announcement that he was keeping Colonsay at the wedding of his second daughter, Kate, to the son of an Edinburgh shipowner. Its timing was as perfect as the occasion, for, in the very best traditions of Colonsay hospitality, every man, woman and child in the community had been invited to the ceilidh-reception in the huge marquee that now adorned the lawn of Colonsay House. There the islanders and the guests, including many who had been flown in by a fleet of light aircraft, danced the night away together in a mood of uninhibited conviviality and togetherness, and all ownership questions and nagging doubts were happily forgotten – if not, when mundane normality returned, entirely answered.

11

HOME IS WHERE THE HEART IS

For so many of those who stepped down the gangway or drove their stuffed-full cars onto the pier, reaching Colonsay was like a homecoming, even if most of them didn't live on the island. A lucky few did have second homes, but the great majority were people, typically families, who came back year after year like returning swallows to a well-loved territory, one that was full of reliable and rewarding inner nourishment. With relief and expectation they would park their pressured mainland lives for a period of restorative island living. They stayed and they re-created: for a week, a fortnight or sometimes longer, mostly staying in one or other of the many holiday houses which the Estate let out. Even if they were setting foot on Colonsay for the first time, the chances were high that they too would fall in love with the place and become regular summer migrants in their turn, quite often such regular ones that their children would return, in the fullness of time, with children of their own to their favoured holiday homes from home.

It was not difficult to see why they kept coming back, for as Professor MacKinnon had observed in the 1880s, 'The island is becoming yearly better appreciated as a health resort and retreat for a quiet holiday. With improved communication it is likely to become more so. For families and especially for children, Colonsay possesses exceptional advantages as a summer residence. Its pure ocean air is unsurpassed and unsurpassable. The island abounds in links well adapted for the game of golf. To one who enjoys a skelping sea, sailing and fishing along the exposed shores are almost always possible during the summer months.

Its numerous reaches of pure sand make it a delightful place for bathing and perfectly safe for children. A general feeling of drowsiness pervades the place. You seem to breathe a delicious narcotic in the balmy salt-sea air. You wish to be alone and you can gratify your wish with ease. Within ten hours sail of Greenock you live for days oblivious of the bustle and strife of the busy world. There is communication with the south twice a week but you wish it was only once.' Not much in this description had changed by the 1970s, except that the ferry now set out from Oban, took two and a half hours and called three times a week instead of two.

Part of the ferry-watching fascination for the locals, including the pier hands, was spotting which old friends of the island came off the boat, and scanning the unrecognised visitors for any clues as to their identity. However, there was a separate category of homecomers who resisted early identification, though they quite often looked annoyingly familiar and would soon enough share their connection and their story. These were the descendants of born and bred Colonsay folk who, many generations previously, had been pressured into quitting their island lives and homes and impelled to find new ones in distant and very different lands.

Colonsay was and is the ancestral home of the Clan MacPhee and the many other variations of that name. The last of the Colonsay MacPhee chiefs was captured and shot in 1623, so the story goes, by a legendary fellow islander by name of *Colla Ciotach*, which means 'left-handed Coll', an ambitious and warlike MacDonald who later came to a sticky end himself. The resulting scattering of the Colonsay MacDuffies and MacPhees only encouraged their deracinated descendants to come to Colonsay from all corners of the globe to establish their personal sense of connection. One frequent returnee was a gentle and generous Swede, called Ulf Macfie Hagman, who organised the repair, re-erection and fencing of *Carragh Mhic a Phie*, 'MacPhee's standing stone', to which the captured MacPhee had been tied and then executed. Another was a determined New Yorker who, had he been clan chief at the time, might well have given

Colla Ciotach a run for his money, for when he stayed at the Hotel he would start each day with an intrepid warrior's breakfast – porridge and crispy bacon, which he mixed together in the one bowl and accompanied with a glass of red wine. To them and the many other visiting MacPhees Colonsay was a kind of spiritual home, no matter how great the differences in context between their lives and those of their forebears might seem to others.

Though these personal journeys of re-connection seemed more acts of imagination than reality, I was fascinated by the evocative stories that were told by some of those island visitors with Colonsay blood in their veins. Such, for example, as the account James S. MacMillan, who was raised in Prince Edward Island on the Atlantic coast of Canada, shared with Big Peter and me in the pottery one August afternoon in 1977. The fact that Peter and I both thought that James bore a striking resemblance to another Colonsay MacMillan, 'The Dan', as Donald MacMillan of Machrins who had died in his nineties a few years earlier was known, only made his story the more compelling.

James' ancestor, Malcolm, then 48 years old, his wife and their four children set sail from Oban in August 1806 on the sailing boat *Spencer*, reaching Charlottetown in the British colony of Prince Edward Island on 22 September that year. Most of the 115 passengers came from Colonsay, it would appear, from the familiar mix of Colonsay surnames in the copy of the copperplate passenger list which was later sent to me – Bells, Munns, MacDuffies, McNeills, Curries and Darrochs amongst others. History remembers them as just one more shipload of 'Selkirk settlers', so named because the passages and grants of land were sponsored by Thomas Douglas, 5th Earl of Selkirk who, on unexpectedly inheriting his father's huge estate, made a philanthropic decision to buy vast acreages in a number of British colonies that are now part of modern Canada in order to help resettle Highland and Island crofters, as well as other poor people from elsewhere in the British Isles who had little land and income and needed to better themselves. The land on Prince

Edward Island was one of his very first major land purchases, and each sponsored family, James told us, was granted 100 acres. The rent for the first three years was three peppercorns per annum while they cleared the virgin land of native forest, sowed and reaped their first crops and built their houses, barns and fences. Thereafter, the rent increased by a few pence each year as each family's wealth increased.

The enormity of the challenges these emigrants faced – and the courage and resolve required to overcome them – put late twentieth-century island problems into perspective. By way of starters, the islanders had to bring themselves to make the huge emotional, as well as practical, decision to leave their island home for ever. Though it is clear that many families consciously decided they would only go if they could go together and be there for each other during the trials ahead, their hearts must have been sore as they turned their eyes for the final time on their island home and friends. Compared to the 2,500-mile sea journey before them, the 32-mile ferry journey to Oban is a relatively insignificant sea crossing, though one which, to this day, regularly challenges and sometimes leaves stormbound a twin-screwed, 3000-ton, all metal CalMac ferry capable of carrying over 60 cars and 500 passengers. The *Spencer*, by contrast, was a 330-ton wooden, three-masted, square-rigged sailing ship which committed itself to facing everything the ocean chose to throw at it over the average journey time of six to eight weeks or so; moreover she was just one of many such overcrowded sailing vessels that carried emigrants from the Highlands and Islands to North America over many decades with, for example, another six sailing from just one neighbouring island – Mull – alone in that selfsame year of 1806. James' family story was that the *Spencer* set out from Oban but was forced back to port three times before she was, at last, able to find a favourable enough wind to begin her vast oceanic crossing, sailing westward past Colonsay on her long, slow journey one last bitter-sweet time.

When, in the 1990s, I had the chance to undertake a bit of research into Canadian Government self-build schemes and contrived to fit Prince Edward Island into my itinerary, I was at last able to visit some of the places where the Colonsay emigrants had made their new homes, lived out their lives and, in due course, been laid to rest. I stayed in a bed and breakfast where, it emerged, my elderly and most hospitable McKinnon hosts were undilutedly Hebridean in their take on life and in most other observable respects except actual residence, so it seemed; in that every single one of their eight great-grandparents, they told me, was the son or daughter of a nineteenth-century emigrant from one Hebridean island or another.

It made me daydream yet again, as I so often did when I lived in Colonsay, about what the island must really have been like to live in when its pre-emigration population was so much larger than the all-time low 120-odd figure it had been whittled away to by the 1970s, each decennial census figure declining remorselessly from its 1841 peak of 936 in Colonsay and 43 in Oronsay. Where had those legions, those boatloads – how many thousands, so many, too many, surely – of Colonsay people gone, during well over a hundred years and more of intermittent but still persistent emigration? To start with in the late eighteenth century, so some of the older islanders and those visiting descendants of emigrants said, they had gone to South Carolina where they were granted tracts of land; then in the first decades of the nineteenth century most went to Woods Island and St Peter's Point, now called Rice Point, in Prince Edward Island; and then during its middle and later decades to Elderslie, Paisley and Collingwood in Ontario, with the earlier Colonsay pioneers clearly sending news and encouragement home to others to follow them out. Some had gone to Australia and New Zealand too, but why had they gone, could they have really stayed and thrived – and did so many really have to go?

I fed my curiosity and sense of the injustice of this by lapping up books like Jim Hunter's mid-seventies landmark, *The Making of the Crofting Community*, which gives its forensic insights into the true stories behind so many forced emigrations from the Highlands and Islands; albeit that the books I read contained very little evidence about what had actually happened on Colonsay. On a couple of occasions when stormbound in Oban, I leafed through late nineteenth-century issues of the *Oban Times* and found reports about Colonsay such as the following from June, 1887. 'Rents on the estate are high even for good times. On farms, rents were recently raised by 30 to 60 per cent; on crofts, by 50 to 100 per cent. 10% reduction on farms and 5% on crofts have been allowed for the last two years on fully paid rents. Rents must be paid in full and to the day otherwise sequestration to the farmer and eviction to the crofter. Tenants struggling under oppressive rents do not find much consideration in offering them bankruptcy and exile as alternatives to penury, nor is there great generosity shown in relieving a tenant of land which you want for yourself and which you have secured before as a successor. The fact is that in this lovely island, more than in most places, it is necessary that the people should assert themselves. They have hitherto shown blind confidence in their rulers and had their reward.' It was an account which squared with those that Neil Martin, *Niall a Goirtein*, born in the early 1890s, told me his grandfather had told him: that, due to his ill health, he had been unable to go on working for the then McNeill lairds as one of their kelp harvesters on remote Seal Island south of Oronsay, so they fined him £2, which was a third of his annual wages, and took his croft from him; the same grandfather who also remembered the day when seventeen families from the southern end of Colonsay emigrated from the island together.

On the other hand, Professor MacKinnon had this to say in his Gaelic essay on Lord Colonsay, Duncan McNeill, who was the island laird from 1844 to 1870, while pursuing a political career which included stints as Solicitor General and Lord Advocate for Scotland for Tory governments of the 1850s and 60s:

When Lord Colonsay got possession of the estate and for many generations before, the situation of the islanders was like that of many other estates that had stayed in the hands of the old Highland families. People were more plentiful than sheep. Rents were not heavy; the island was fertile, renowned for its potatoes and black cattle. Colonsay was a place in which a family could be raised for very little. The rent would be paid with kelp and a stirk and the family would live on a little meal and a lot of potatoes, butter and milk. Some will say that the Gael was happy then, when the population was plentiful, sheep scarce and houses and roads as may be. Others will say that the people of the Highlands and Islands at this time were slaves, in an intolerable situation for a free people, under the authority and power of an individual who was their Lord and master. It is my opinion that there is a little truth in both views but this is a broad question on which people's opinions may change once they have thought about it.

A year or two after Lord Colonsay got the estate came the potato failure, an affair of great moment for many landlords especially in the Highlands and Islands. The population was numerous and their livelihood was very quickly cut away. A large sum of money was raised throughout the Kingdom to feed the people who were dying of starvation. On some of the estates the poor people were swept away mercilessly to the cities and foreign countries. On others, the Landlords, at great cost to themselves, kept the people alive and won great respect throughout the land for their generosity. On the small estate of Colonsay the laird took a different approach to these distressing times. He did not believe that it was the right thing to support idle people. He was too proud to take help from strangers; he was too decent to drive the inhabitants away although this was his hard task. A decrease in the population was needed by the people and the laird but it was right and proper that the decrease should be effected with patience and care.

When Lord Colonsay took over the Estate, there weren't any roads, the houses were in a bad state and agricultural practice was very backward. The numerous population – in my opinion too numerous – was measurably happy but most were in bad circumstances. Twenty years later there was not an estate between Cape Wrath and the Mull of Kintyre where a visitor would see more signs of comfort amongst its inhabitants. During this period many emigrated to foreign countries – especially to Canada; but this was remarkable about the emigrations from Colonsay that there was not one person who left the island against his will, that the majority went at the expense of the laird; and although today [i.e. the 1870s] there are more Colonsay folk living away from the island than living on it, those that left and those that remain have the same respect for the gentleman who was their laird.

Respect for lairds and professors notwithstanding, the longer I lived in Colonsay the more I wondered how much better life might have been for our island community had the resident population remained significantly bigger, and whether it could be increased again so that more people – especially young couples, families with children like ourselves – could make good homes for themselves on the island as we had done, and otherwise add to the life of this genuinely isolated but still precious and interesting little community. But therein lay a dilemma: where would they live?

Of the Estate's sixty-odd houses on the island a third were used to provide holiday homes and, the way I saw and felt it then, these were houses which had provided permanent homes until not that long ago when the 'New Laird' had fulfilled the promise he had given the islanders on opening a 'Sale of Work' in the Village Hall shortly after his father had died. The latest hereditary title-holder in the continuing line of Lord Strathconas and Mount Royals said that, regrettably, he could not afford to go on 'mollycoddling' the islanders as his father had done by employing so many of them in Estate jobs which simply didn't come anywhere near paying for themselves. So, the jobs duly went and the former Estate workers and their families had little other realistic option but to leave the island, with surely similar anxieties to those emigrants of old, to find new employers and make new lives and homes for themselves elsewhere. Their former homes became just cleared and empty properties again – 'voids' as they are called in the housing trade, although 'devoids' might have described them better – and could now be let out, or very occasionally sold, as holiday accommodation, which generated much greater levels of rental and other income plus all the savings to the balance account from not having to pay any wages to the departed. Though the in-migrant family in Glen Cottage was a very lucky and rare exception to this unsentimental, profit and loss approach to estate management, its so-called breadwinner harboured few doubts and quite a lot of frustration that it was short-sighted; although it is also true to say that, many years later, he came to adjust his view – somewhat.

The adjustment began very slowly when, as the Professor had suggested, I began to think a bit more about the bigger picture and, it went without saying, chew it over with Big Peter in one of our regular dialogues. Why, we wondered, didn't the island have a few council houses like most other small communities: that would surely help address the housing problem? We soon had the chance to share our thoughts with the Chief Executive of Argyll and Bute District Council, Michael Gossip, who came over to Colonsay one hot July with our local Councillor, Frank Spears, irrepressible proprietor of the Port Askaig Hotel in the neighbouring island of Islay. They asked us to come with them on a drive round the island in Frank's car and have a chat about the issues they wanted discussed at the inaugural meeting of the newly established Colonsay Community Council, of which we and five other locals found ourselves the first members. Our first stop was overlooking Kiloran Bay, where we got out to admire its picture-postcard perfection and feel the baking sunshine. 'Now then, first things first,' Frank said, opening the boot to reveal a carefully prepared minibar in cardboard boxes, with almost as good a selection as was on offer at the Port Askaig Hotel itself. 'Would anyone care for a refreshment?' It would have been discourteous to refuse, especially in such warm weather, and the candid discussion which followed was only interrupted by further pit stops to take in other points of interest, as well as such occasional refreshment as the prevailing weather conditions seemed to dictate.

On getting some council houses, the Chief Executive was surprisingly forthright: Yes, we will provide them if the local need is demonstrated; and don't ever forget, he added pointedly, that local authorities have powers of compulsory purchase where landowners might be unwilling to make land – or even empty estate houses if that seems the better solution – available to help meet locally identified needs; and, he concluded quite matter-of-factly, we would not hesitate to use those powers should the need arise. All this came as a total revelation and no little astonishment to the men who worked on the pier, and also made me start wondering about what the future might hold for Colonsay. I was beginning to wonder too where my own future might lie, as I grew more and more interested and involved in island community development matters, not least the aspect of affordable housing to meet local needs which I was just beginning to grasp was not only to do with existing supply but with new supply as well. A seed had been sown.

Good as his executive word, Michael Gossip lost no time in discussing the council housing possibilities with the Laird and, on the basis of identified local housing needs, was able to persuade the Estate to sell the Council four of its empty houses at Glassard; four of those very same houses that an earlier Lord Strathcona had generously built over half a century earlier to help resettle the isolated and poorly housed Riasg Buidhe folk – the choice seemed appropriate. As one of the local households who had filled in an application form to express their housing need, the Alexanders were in due course offered one of the Glassard council houses; an offer they eventually declined, mostly on the grounds that home is where the heart is and ours was in Glen Cottage: for although it was really too small for the five of us, it was cosy and had layers of Hebridean charm and homeliness embedded within its thick stone walls. However, the process forced us to think about where we, as a family, might really want to make another home. Another seed had been sown.

Meantime, I remained 'the potter', as reliant as any full-time islander on the seasonal visitors who came happily to their holiday homes and then came to me looking for a souvenir to take back to their permanent ones. Pleased as I was to see them, by the time September came around and all the schools, first the Scottish ones and then the English, had gone back and the last of the holidaying families with them, I felt relieved to see them go and feel the island getting back to 'normal'. Colonsay returned to its essential self, home to the permanent community with all its year-round social and economic survival needs and interdependencies, and upon whose well-being both its permanent and holidaying residents, including the local landowner, depended if the island home we shared was to remain a viable as well as a welcoming one. Nevertheless, after a long, quiet winter I was only too happy to dump purist for tourist, and welcome back the seasonal visitors with hardly any ambivalence of my own.

12

THE POTTER'S WHEEL

My daily commute from Glen Cottage to the pottery was less than a hundred yards.

In the morning, not usually first thing, I would don my clay-smeared potter's smock, fill up my big white-enamelled pitcher with water from the big Windsor sink in the kitchen, making sure it was good and warm if I was going to do some throwing, as the pottery had no heating until Big Peter, who had also felt its wintertime chill, donated a tiny but effective coal-burning stove which he had rescued from the back of a shed somewhere.

I would make my way through the garden gate, chasing the more unruly of our chickens back out onto their hen-hut side of the fence; past the walled yard called the 'Coal Ree' where the coal and Calor Gas cylinders were stored; past the now superseded Hillman Minx which had settled comfortably into the grass and made a favourite outdoor playroom for the children (until the Laird suggested, to my chagrin, though not unreasonably in the circumstances, that both the time and the vehicle, which appeared to have acquired some kind of fungal infection on its exterior and had clumps of vegetation growing out of the dashboard, were now ripe for a final journey to the island's dump); past the old, stone-built storehouse which had been erected by the eighteenth and nineteenth-century McNeill lairds who preceded the Strathconas and which was now used as an agricultural supplies depot, called the Islay Farmers Store (that would be opened up on request by 'Foelallie' McNeill, our incomparable babysitter); across the track that led up to Hazel Cottage next door where Foelallie lived with her sister

Catriona, Catriona's husband Finlay and their four fun sons, Dondie, Johnny, Donald and wee Finlay, a household that made the best neighbours anyone could have hoped for; past *Tobair a Charpenter*, the 'Carpenter's Well', tucked away just below the Hazel Cottage road which we still used when our water supply ran dry and which I still drained, scrubbed and painted with white lime once a year to keep the water sparkling clean; past the boathouse loft accessed by an external flight of stone steps which the Gaelic-speaking islanders called *Lobhta Charpenter,* the 'Carpenter's Loft', and which the Laird and his evergreen boatman, Dougie McGillvray, used as the Estate's boat-repair shed; past the shingle shore of the harbour which our hens were usually busy scratching and probing for the grit and the insects which gave their eggs yolks of such rich orange and flavour, and where a pair of ringed plovers would make their invisible nest in the springtime; and, finally, take the last few paces over the greensward, past its motley collection of small boats pulled up for the winter, and into the boathouse which now had a large arched kiln built out of white insulation bricks at its far end, pots in various stages of preparation on shelves alongside the walls and a potter's kickwheel underneath a skylight.

On a good or half-decent morning, which it was more often than not, the first act of my working day was to prop the smaller of the double doors wide open to let the daylight and any subsequent visitors in, albeit that my regulars were not easily deterred by a sometimes furtively shut door if they detected any telltale signs of life behind it.

It was a journey which could take 30 seconds, or at least as many minutes depending on the human traffic I encountered along the way. 'Watty', Walter Williams, might well be the other side of the Coal Ree wall, taking a breather from shovelling coal or loading gas cylinders into his red trailer for tractor-hauled delivery around the island. Foelallie could easily be chatting to customers in the Islay Farmers Store or Dougie might be having a quiet smoke of one of his record-breaking series of roll-ups in his black baby Austin parked on the grass below the Carpenter's Loft.

Whoever was about, Colonsay custom and good manners dictated that passing the time of day should be neither dodged nor rushed. For, unless the circumstances were exceptional, life was too short to do otherwise; and why miss the opportunity to catch up with island news and the various local takes upon it, without which it would be impossible to reach an informed understanding?

Though I could hardly claim that I was buckling under unduly stressful commuting or work pressures, pot production levels somehow never reached their potential. True, I was all too readily diverted by visitors, whether my regular locals or my tourist-season visitors, many of whom came back year after year to add still more pieces to their catalogue of purchases – and some of whom, like the lovely and irrepressible Leahy sisters, Paddy and Cathy, who had a much-frequented second home on the island, should really have been awarded controlling shares in the business, such a volume of fired ceramic did they generously relieve me of over the years, and carry back with them to the mainland.

True, too, that the potter was all too often self-diverted by his inescapable escapist tendencies, which translated into 'gone awol, pursuing other interests' and a genuinely closed door with absolutely nothing at all going on behind it while he was absent. Nevertheless, authentic studio potter I became, as I applied myself, week in, week out, to the rhythmic cycle and the unavoidable discipline of the age-old craft, and through constant repetition and practice learnt the skills and requirements of my trade properly – wedging and kneading the clay; making the lumps on the whirring potter's wheel burgeon into whichever form of domestic utensil I had set myself to make that day; trimming and turning footrings into the pots another day after they had dried just enough to 'leather hardness'; making and attaching handles and spouts as required; carefully packing as much into the kiln as was possible once the pots were bone dry, 'biscuit'-firing them so that they became hard but still porous; then double-dipping each piece in the creamy liquid glaze, making sure to wax-resist their undersides and flanges; decorating the dry-coated pots with quickly executed, oxide-laden brushstrokes and, finally, packing the kiln again for the final 'glaze'-firing, taking care that the pots weren't so close as to stick to each other once the glaze was made molten by the firing, while trying at the same time to ensure that as many pots of differing shapes and sizes were placed as carefully and space-efficiently as possible on the successively mounted kiln shelves.

Though, regrettably, I never ever earned enough money from making my pots, the process brought other rewards. It did a lot to settle my tendency for debilitating inner wheesht, bringing resolution to insistent self-doubts and insecurities for at least as long as I remained absorbed by the task in front of me. 'Throwing' pots was, almost always – there were days though – truly therapeutic: at its best, body and mind would be as perfectly centred as the clay on the kick-wheel, and an acute sense of control and touch would pour out effortlessly through the ends of one's fingers. I liked to throw thin-sectioned, non-chunky pots, and the greater inherent strength of stoneware clay allowed me to practise as I preferred. My favourite test of skill and creativity was to throw large, generous and continuously curved (no straight bits permitted) bowls with a well-defined lip, and into the basal trunk of which I would later turn a deep foot-ring before incising it underneath, as I did to all my pots, with 'Colonsay Pottery' and the year of its making. Though it felt deeply satisfying when, seemingly out of nothing, I conjured up something pleasing to the senses in both form and decoration, I found the steady craftsmanship side of the process at least as satisfying as when I was making sure, for example, that the handle I was attaching to a mug or a teapot would never come away later in its user's hand – a principle which stood me in good stead when I applied it with the same care and attention to detail in subsequent lines of work.

However, every potter has to face his regular moments of truth, and these were the firings, the baking of the pots in my hand-built kiln. I was making stoneware pottery, which is harder and more durable than earthenware, though both types need two firings in the kiln – the biscuit and the glaze. If you haven't prepared the clay you used to make your pot or clay object with properly and it has an air bubble in it, then it may well crack or explode the first time you fire it, and the same can happen if it still contains moisture and you heat the kiln up too quickly – the proof of the pudding is in the care that goes into its making and its cooking. Provided your pots pass their biscuit-firing exam they can then be dipped and decorated and packed into the kiln for their glaze-firing which, for stoneware, means reaching a much higher temperature of almost 1300 degrees centigrade – a fiercely bright, orangey-white heat when what till then looks little different from dried emulsion is transmogrified into glistening, molten glass on the sides of the pots.

My five-foot-high kiln was fired by two big and, as the power was gradually turned up, increasingly noisy gas burners, and took somewhere between fourteen and twenty watchful and broody hours, depending on the wind direction and the flow of air through the downdraft kiln, to bring up to the maximum temperature where I would then hold it for some time for a good 'soak', so making sure that the molten glaze completed its melting process properly.

The unrelenting roar of the blue-flamed burners going full blast, the dazzling glints and gleams of the orange-white heat through the cracks of the overlapping kiln bricks and the wall of heat that now filled the pottery always made this the most dramatic and nerve-racking time in the whole pot-making cycle, from its wet clay lump birthing to its glazed completion as a finished object ready for an independent life of its own. At this culminating point of the firing process I would go round to the back of the kiln and push in the damper a bit, till the flames started to turn from orange to yellow and push back through the cracks in the kiln bricks, so as to achieve a 'reduction' in the glazes and decorations on the pots – the alteration that takes place in their chemical structures when you force the naked flames to suck oxygen from their oxides because the air supply in the furnace is no longer available. The colours of the glazes and, in particular, of the differing oxide brushstrokes applied, are irreversibly altered by this 'reduction' process in unique and often unanticipated and beautiful ways. It is an essential part of the magic and mystery of working with flame-fired stoneware and I was in its thrall.

One last look through the the spy-holes – wedge-shaped slivers of kiln bricks – at the pyrometric cones strategically placed on kiln shelves which, when they bent over, would prove that the top, middle and bottom of the kiln had come up to temperature – and I would switch off the burners and close off the gas cylinders. If I had packed the kiln in the morning it would be late at night, often the wee small hours, when the firing would finish; and there would be a dreamlike quality to the sudden silence, the still mesmerising presence of the potent and pulsating kiln – full of my now transformed pots, but impossible at this still brightly glowing stage to discern whether good, bad or boring. It was all over till the next time and, eventually and rather reluctantly, I would meander back to the cottage in the darkness with all the world abed, and only me and my pottery aware of the climactic drama we had just shared.

It was with a mixture of excitement and trepidation that, many hours later after the kiln had been allowed to cool down properly, I would remove and stack all the bricks from the front wall of the kiln and carefully begin to unpack it and inspect the results of the firing, shelf by shelf, pot by precious pot. I always had the pottery door firmly shut for this bit of the process: this was personal and private, just the potter and his pots. There was the agony of the disaster – a big plate perhaps, always difficult to fire evenly using a naked flame, with a heat crack in it – and, just occasionally, there was the intimate thrill of seeing something for the first time which takes you by surprise and makes your heart miss a beat, maybe a nicely-thrown and well-turned fruit bowl with a rich and unblemished glaze and some passable Chinese-y brushwork to which the reduction firing had added some unexpectedly beautiful colour transformations – burnished, glinting coppers, say, emerging out of deep cobalt blues.

Generally though, my main feeling was of sheer relief if the rest of the workaday pots had fired well and looked good enough to be put on the shelves for sale, or packed up and despatched as orders to waiting customers. That they sold too well and too quickly for my liking only proves how just unbusinesslike that Colonsay potter was. At the height of the summer season my momentarily replenished stock would be consumed within days of my unpacking the kiln and expectant holiday visitors would have to content themselves with looking at the unfired pots as they started to accumulate again on the shelves or with placing orders for later collection or transhipment.

Though I much enjoyed seeing and re-seeing my tourist season visitors, people from every airt and sundry walks of life who wended their way round the harbour shore to the door of the pottery, I was always relieved when September came round again and the last of them had made their return ferry journeys to resume their mainland lives. My regular island visitors would revert again confidently to their usual winter visiting routines, knowing that they would have the undivided attention of the potter when they called. When they weren't there, I could stand absent-mindedly at the door of the pottery again without fear of being caught out while I watched my small slice of island world going through its unremarkable, but to me spirit-soothing, daily changes: the ebb and flow of the tides; an otter or a cormorant fishing busily in the filling harbour, even, during the wintertime and early spring, the goose-sized great northern diver, who spent most of his time feeding far off-shore, but seemed to like coming in from time to time for a bit of hard-earned respite; the fishing boat approaching the end of the pier and me trying to discern whether it was Ross McMahon from Kerrera with his lobster creels or an east coast trawler laying up for the night; wondering if I needed some more hot water before I started throwing again, and even if I didn't I could do with a cup of tea. And better take my binocs with me, as I suddenly thought I was due for a quick run in the car up to my one of my favourite birdwatching points at *Laonairigh* (Projecting rock shieling), above Loch Fada. Normal pottery service had, thank heavens, been resumed.

13

WHEN THE BOAT COMES IN

My regular, almost daily, visitors to the pottery all lived within easy walking distance and usually popped in on their way to or from the shop and post office. I had less regular ones too who lived in other parts of the island, but who might well call in if they were stopping to collect something from the Islay Farmers Store and, if they spotted that another islander like Big Peter was already down visiting, the chances were high that they would come down to see what was doing and get the 'craic'.

I was pleased, only a few months after moving to Colonsay, to receive a rare visit from Donald 'Gibby', who lived on his Kilchattan croft on the west side but worked as the island's piermaster and self-employed lobster fisherman from the pier and harbour that the pottery looked out upon. I was a bit taken aback, though, when he told that me that he would soon be moving to Fionnphort at the furthest end of the Ross of Mull to take up a new job as the skipper of the busy CalMac ferry boat that safely collected and returned its endless stream of visitors to the magical island of Iona, drawn there by its famous saint, Columba. I was really surprised though when he asked me if I would be interested in working on the pier after he had left to take up his new responsibilities, and Big Peter had stepped up to become Colonsay's new piermaster. There was some logic to it: no one lived nearer the pier than me, and I was otherwise deemed young and fit and able enough to become Peter's assistant for a job which, in essence, only required the postholder to turn out three times a week, weather permitting, for short periods of concentrated labour.

I had little hesitation in saying yes, as the extra and regular £10 a week would be decidedly handy, though I did wonder whether the island would burst out laughing at my lack of credentials the first time I stood on the pier in my new incarnation. Big Peter offered rather less fulsome reassurance than I was hoping for – 'Ach, all you've got to do is catch the rope, potter' – but the reality was that the islanders saw little amiss in the sometimes strange coupling, or even tripling or quadrupling, of different part-time jobs, for it was what lots of islanders had to do, duly did and still do to make up a composite living wage.

I quickly came to enjoy my new role once I had literally learnt the ropes – catching the thin cord heaving line with its heavy 'monkey's head' ball at the end, which would be thrown towards the pier by one of the sailors standing on the approaching ship's prow; my job being to catch it and then haul it, and the much heavier mooring rope to which the line was tied, as quickly as I could onto the pier, before dropping its eye over the furthest forward bollard-cleat. Then returning quickly to catch the second proferred rope, the 'spring line', which I would drop over another bollard much further back along the pier, the one secured rope counterbracing the other. When Big Peter had done the same with the stern ropes at the head of the pier, the sailors would use the ship's capstans to pull the boat tight into the side of the pier ready for safe disembarkation.

In wild weather, when gale-force winds could quickly catch and twist the bow of the ferry as she lost forward motion on the final few yards of her approach, the acts of throwing and catching the heaving line and getting at least one rope locked onto its bollard could take on a frantic degree of urgency, lest the ferry get too close to the adjacent rocky shore and the skipper would have to put her full astern, abort the landing attempt and try again. Though some days it felt more like I was tethering the island to the ferry than the ferry to the island it made no difference: I just relished it, most of the time, dressed in my yellow oilskins, clay-streaked 'bullseye' wellies and faded cream woollen titfer, ready for anything the weather could summon, and happy to be playing my bit part in the thrice-weekly drama that accompanied the coming and going of the island's lifeline.

Between securing and letting go the ropes there was much work to be done. Peter and I would manhandle the heavy wooden – later, lighter aluminium – gangway to its position below whichever deck and exit the height of the tide suggested foot passengers should disembark from. The sailors would hoist the gangway into position, exchange a wisecrack or two with the pier hands below, and the pedestrian exodus from the ship's flank would begin; the latest mix of familiar and unfamiliar faces, whether, after a rough crossing, looking a touch peelie-wallie and mightily relieved to be setting foot on terra firma again, or, after a smoother one, simply happy to have reached their home or holiday destination, their heads looking round expectantly for their reception parties.

After which we would turn our attention to the unloading of cars and cargo – then a less than straightforward affair. When, in 1973, CalMac decided to change its traditional ferry route to Colonsay from its distant and relatively remote pier on West Loch Tarbert on the Mull of Kintyre to the new and much more direct crossing from the bustling port of Oban, it did so knowing that Colonsay would have to exchange its modernised ferry, the *Arran* – with its hoist-loading lift, which allowed cars and wheeled cages of cargo to be driven from its side-loading ramp straight onto the pier – for an older relation from a previous era, when all cargo, including the occasional car, had to be lowered into the hold through a hatchway in the foredeck.

So, unloading the ship's cargo involved opening up the hatches and hoisting everything in and out on the ship's derrick, a fixed crane which paid out a metal line with a great big iron hook at the end. The wheeled cages were hitched up and swung ashore, plonking down on the pier without too much difficulty unless there was a swell running, when the landing could be anything but smooth. To get the cages into the dry of the shed we would hitch them on to the 'iron horse', a dark-green, three-wheeled, Iron Age survivor that, with some luck and effort, could be cranked into feisty, diesel-fumed life, and which it seemed CalMac had kindly awarded Colonsay as a kind of consolation prize. After trying it out first, Peter didn't hesitate in appointing me as designated driver, and it soon became clear that this still game museum piece had dodgy brakes and would occasionally stick in gear, sending innocent bystanders scuttling for cover as I wrestled the brute to a halt by driving it into a bollard and switching off its engine.

Loading and unloading cars required a lot more care. Industrial-strength cushions were strategically deployed to make sure that the metal nets that went under the two sets of wheels didn't mark or damage the car when the derrick took up its weight and gingerly hoisted it out of the ship's hold onto the pier, though there were always other willing hands to help the pier workers make sure that the vehicle had a happy landing. It all took time and hardly fitted the roro (roll on/roll off) description – more nororo – and when, late on a Friday afternoon, at the height of the summer tourist season, the old and well-loved *Claymore* would call in at Colonsay packed, so it seemed, to the gunwales with one lot of summer visitors arriving to spend their weeks-long holidays on the island, but with an equal number waiting patiently to make their return journey home again, Peter and I would feel that we had been well-worked after, on top of the record number of cages crammed to overflowing with cardboard boxes full of supplies for the shop, plus innumerable lifesaving barrels of beer for the Hotel, we had carefully landed and de-netted the ten or eleven cars – the *Claymore*'s maximum complement – that were carefully winched out of the ship's hold and then we'd done it all again in reverse with the same number. Little wonder that the old *Claymore* always ran late on a 'change-over' Friday, but it was some show she put on, nevertheless, on a warm summer's evening as she lay alongside in the sunshine, untroubled by all the colourful hustle and bustle of the frenetic pier, that most graceful and accommodating old lady from a less pressured age, loved and admired by all.

Within a few years, though, the old *Claymore* had been retired from the CalMac fleet and sold to the Greeks for a silver-painted makeover and Mediterranean swansong. Her thankfully side-loading replacement, the MV *Columba*, nowadays reincarnated as a 5-star luxury cruise ship fittingly renamed the *Hebridean Princess*, took up the Oban-Colonsay run, supposedly arriving at ten in the evening in the summer season and lying over at the pier two nights a week, before setting sail at six o' clock sharp the next morning. I became her nightwatchman, if only to avoid having to get up again so soon after eventually getting to bed, and increased my CalMac wage packet by another fiver a night. Save for John Gallagher the night steward from Barra and, every now and then, an insomniac skipper in pyjamas, slippers and dressing gown, the boat was all mine to keep an eye on while the crew and passengers slept in their cabins.

When I wasn't playing cards with John, I would read a book or wander the decks, keeping one eye on the ropes and gangway as the tide rose or fell, and the other on the lookout for a late returner from the Hotel who might well be grateful for a helping hand aboard. In my mind's eye I'm leaning on the deckrail again and gazing back at those familiar moonlit landmarks and silhouetted outlines of the sleeping Scalasaig glen, my home patch, where the dreamlike quality of those sometimes perfectly still summer nights would only be fractured by the occasional outburst of shrill piping from enamoured oystercatchers or the curious rasping and thrumming sounds that came from the snipe, strafing their bogland territories. From my upper-deck vantage points I witnessed night-time wonders too – a cascading shower of shooting stars that I thought would never end and, on another night, an impossibly acrobatic otter endlessly pursuing a shoal of quicksilver squid which, so it seemed, had become mesmerised in a deep pool of liquefied luminescence on the *Columba*'s seaward side, cast by a decklight that someone had forgotten to extinguish.

It was a long night to stay awake through, though, and it was probably only the breakfast that John cooked specially for the two of us about half past four in the morning, before he made the sailors theirs, that kept me going: it was a mouth-watering, cholesterol-filled feast of a 'full Scottish' breakfast which probably advanced my present tablet-taking requirement, by at least a decade. Dawn comes early in the summertime north and I would watch the big, red sun rise majestically from behind the Isles of the Sea (aka the Garvellachs) and the mainland mountains beyond. Not long after, Peter would have arrived back down at the pier in his van looking short of sleep and, after giving me his usual ironic early morning greeting, *'Well, a Photter, dh'eiridh thu'*, 'Well, Potter, you got up', the pair of us would stand waiting for the sailors to unhitch their end of the gangway so that we could then move on to our respective ends of the pier and cast off the ropes.

Not, however, before those on duty had, all too often, witnessed the last rites and tearful conclusions of yet another holiday romance, the shared poignancy of whose heartfelt moments only wearing thin as the long, summer season approached its end; for while you would need to have been born with a heart of stone not to feel for the departing lassies, your feelings for the home-grown Hebridean charmers seeing them off were likely to become more mixed as you remembered the times you had seen their familiar faces that summer season, saying the same sincere farewells to their succession of holiday sweethearts. Sadder by far, though, were those ungodly hour embarkations of the island's youngsters, making their way back to secondary school and hostel accommodation in Oban after one of their rare visits home during term time, for their half-term break and a long weekend in between – if they had been lucky and not been further confined to their mainland barracks by a stormbound ferry. Though this aspect of the education system was fairly stoically accepted by those parents and children who could do little to avoid it, there was no love lost for it either, and real tears were regularly shed by both parties. When, every now and then, a young islander threw a last minute tantrum and point-blank refused to make the walk up the wretched gangplank, I wasn't the only adult present moved to secretly support the rebellion, even if you tried not to show it and so make the situation worse.

With the ferry heading back to Oban and the pier left to the seagulls once more, the question was whether to go back to bed for a few hours or try to keep going. In the Hebrides a decision deferred still counts as a decision and, in any case, mine would usually be taken for me by a now thoroughly wide-awake Big Peter, whose engaged and engaging mind would be ready for another day's conversation. As soon as the boat had sailed we would jump into his van, and he would pull in by the island's one and only red telephone kiosk to let me hop over the garden fence, his intention being to carry on up the road to the GPO 'radio station' where his other job began, mine being to try and catch up on some sleep before venturing down to the pottery. More often than not, though, we would sit there blethering till island life started up properly for the day.

Always first to come on the scene would be Mary Clark, who would walk down the hotel brae from her little cottage on the knoll above to collect the couple of cows from *pàirc a chlada-ich,* 'the shore field', and then walk them slowly back up the hill past the Hotel to Scalasaig Farm, where they would be milked by her nephew, John. The courtesies of those fresh mornings would be exchanged, and in no time at all Peter would have evinced Mary's gently tinkling laughter with one or more of his wry-to-scurrilous observations on island life, past or present. If we were still blethering when my neighbour Finlay drove past in the Estate pick-up on his way to work, then we knew it must be eight o'clock and time to go about our separate businesses.

There were other boats too, cargo boats like the *Glenlight* and the *Loch Carron* which appeared at unpredictable times, if not out of a clear blue sky then likely a windier and greyer one, to deliver coal and Calor Gas cylinders or to take sheep or cattle from the island to the sales in Oban, though livestock was some- times added to the regular ferry cargo if car traffic was light. In any event, loading livestock was invariably a challenging affair, particularly when the poor animals had to be loaded onto the maindeck or into the hold below via an extra long gangway used for the purpose. Sheep were only easier to manage because they were smaller and usually capable of some manhandling in close combat situations, although it was much easier to lose one that was making a bid for freedom, particularly en route from the holding pens opposite Glen Cottage at the bottom of the road that led onto the pier. However, once the first one had been persuaded onto the gangway, the rest would usually follow in sheepish solidarity.

Cattle could be a lot more stubborn and difficult, however. Apart from any other bovine considerations, the gangway must have seemed impossibly narrow to them, and I am ashamed to this day at the way I inadvertently let out a strangled laugh as one island farmer received a frightened response from the rear end of a resistant cow, to which he was applying all his remaining bodily strength to try to shove onto the gangway. The look of bespattered reproach which that particular farmer, the very gentlest and nicest of islanders, gave me for my bad manners lives with me to this day. Occasionally, however, we would also welcome one or two immigrants bringing new blood to the island stock, and never was any visitor to Colonsay more respectfully received than when a huge bull was landed and, held by no more than a short rope threaded through a ring in the end of its nose, led by an intrepid farmer into the float waiting to carry it to its new island home. Though they always seemed to be the most docile of big beasts, it was a task that I never once felt the need to volunteer for.

If a Ph.D thesis on the importance of ferries in island psychology has not yet been produced, then it surely deserves to be. In Colonsay each coming and going of the ferry seemed like an episode in a drama serial to which every last one of us was addicted, whether we were there to see it for ourselves or were asking for news about it later from eye-witnesses. Big Peter's story about old *Ruaridh Hearach*, 'Roger from Harris', summed it up. One of Peter's several roles underpinning the cycle of island life was to help provide local undertaker services; and, in this unsung hero capacity, he had been asked to go and measure up Ruaridh who had, Peter was sadly informed, just passed away. On reaching the bedside and bending over the mortal remains to respectfully begin his task, Peter was somewhat taken aback to see the alleged deceased open his eyes and ask the question that was uppermost in his mind, 'Did the boat come, *a Pharuig* [Peter]?' . On regaining his composure, Peter was particularly pleased to be able to reassure a still very much alive Ruaridh that it had, and then to give him a satisfactorily detailed account of all the day's comings and goings at the pier.

It was on those days when it was touch and go whether the ferry would set out from Oban or not or, when it did, whether it would be forced back by the storm-driven seas that the psychological impact would be felt most keenly. During some winter periods the weather could have been so persistently wild that the ferry would have missed consecutive sailings, and the collective willpower of the island would be focused on telekinetically prising the ferry away from its mainland berth and dragging it towards the island, almost regardless of the weather conditions. It was then critically important to know who the skipper was, and the answer every islander wanted to hear was 'It's the Gunner', for Captain Donald Gunn was universally credited with being the least easily deterred of the several skippers who, on a rotating basis, took charge of the ferry. It was the Gunner who had the record of bringing the ferry and its human and other cargo safely home when most islanders would think twice about going out of doors, let alone going to sea. So, if the Gunner concluded that he couldn't come then no one doubted that the seas really were too difficult to countenance; if it was one of the other skippers, then stories would be swapped about ferry journeys made or abandoned under their command, and unfavourable judgements made as to how they compared on the Gunner scale when the going got tough.

On such tense and usually long days when one could think of little else but the ferry, I would stand on the knoll behind the pottery and scan the seas with my binoculars, sometimes catching the first glimpse of a distant speck near the far off Gar-vellach Isles, other times being completely taken by surprise as she suddenly hove into view, looking huge and very close, less than a mile away in fact, having hugged the sheltered lee of the island to emerge dramatically from behind the point at Glassard. Then it would be a mad dash to get down to the end of the pier to meet her in time, and though there was no round of applause the universal sense of gratitude as she tied up alongside was pal-pable. The crew would be looking quietly satisfied too, for they were generally all, ship's officers and sailors, Gaelic-speaking, Hebridean islanders themselves, and knew from both upbring-ing and profession what being on the end of a much-delayed ferry arrival really meant for a small island community. Big Peter would share a *'Brios maith seolaidh'* or two by way of comment on the weather, and all present would share the sense of relief that this cliffhanger of a page had at last been turned in the never ending drama of when the boat comes in. Even if they hadn't been there to see it themselves, almost every living soul in the island would soon feel the better of hearing about the very latest episode.

14

FAMILY MATTERS

If men mature too slowly then I was no exception. The extra six years I had lived on planet Earth compared to my sweetheart counted for nothing, except that I had had more time to indulge myself. I was, after all, art-school trained, and all those hours spent in The Leather Bottle at the end of Merton Hall Road, London SW19, had done little to help, albeit that, when not in the College local, I had somehow found enough time to acquire the basic skills of an old-fashioned trade and with it the bottom layer of the self-belief needed to help me grow up – eventually.

We were both very young when we first set eyes on each other, Jane just nineteen, myself only numerically older. Barely fifteen months had passed between our summer idyll in Carsaig and coming to Colonsay with our baby boy to set up home as the newest and least experienced of island families. Glen Cottage felt like it understood as it offered up its quiet embrace and made us feel that we belonged there. Money and material possessions were scarce, but we really didn't care. One large and very comfy old armchair in front of the open fire, more than big enough for two plus a wee one, or even two or three, to snuggle up on, stood in the way of our non-existent ambition for a three-piece suite, and our visitors made do, equally happily it seemed, sitting on kitchen chairs around Madam Doubtfire's oak table with a mug of tea. A full-blown westerly howling down the Scalasaig glen, driving horizontal rain and hailstones onto the living-room window panes, making a noise like a drum roll on a snare drum, only made it feel cosier and more intimate. The walls were three feet thick and we had our love to keep us warm in our new but comfortingly old-fashioned home.

Either side of the front door the world was full of discoveries: mostly happy, some disconcerting. Outside, the shock of realisation that came after putting a big, wellied foot in it, especially in the early days when we were getting to know island ways and local politics, was only topped by the hot flushes of mortification which followed later. Soon all parties got to know and understand each other better and, in any case, islanders were very forgiving of those who were unmistakably green and innocent.

Inside the four walls family life, with all its comforting norms, became established. Somehow the nappy bucket, that almost constant companion, springs instantly to mind. Disposable nappies were an unreliable and expensive option when you lived on a remote island, and like most we depended on rotating the traditional, flannelette variety. Held at arms length between thumb and forefinger, the used nappies would be gingerly plopped into a plastic bucket to join the others for a cold stew in a watery brine that had been fortified with Napisan, a product that promised to be kind to babies' bottoms, though it still managed to bring tears to the eyes. When its lid would no longer stay down the bucket would be upended into one of our deep double Windsor kitchen sinks, and whoever's turn it was – 'your turn, surely?' – would rub, wring, rinse and repeat until the whole lot could be pegged out on the washing line like a very long strip of celebratory bunting. In wet weather the nappies would join everything else hanging on the 'maiden', the clothes pulley over the living-room fire, and in front of which our succession of island babies had their bums cleaned, tummies tickled and nappies changed.

Forty-odd years later, I discover that not just those old showstoppers, oestrogen and testosterone, but a cocktail of even more hormones was mixing it in the bloodstream of our shared young lives, secretly influential most of the time, but erupting now and then as they made their feelings better known – as if there weren't enough other influences, conscious and covert, to be contending with. My unwise suggestion that Jane's occasional bouts of tiredness and unhappiness at the end of our first winter on the island could just be put down to 'hormones' turned out to be about as right as I was decidedly wrong to mention it. The tests which came back from the doctor explained that we had a baby on the way – the second of four such total surprises who somehow made it to adulthood. He also advised that island mothers-to-be did not have their babies at home but were expected to take the ferry to the maternity hospital in Oban in advance of the due time, because it reduced the childbirth risks for all concerned.

Fair enough, except that no one had told the baby. And so it was that late one Monday morning in early September I took our Danny, not yet one and a half, in his pushchair up the single-track road to Glassard and the island's shop, post office and petrol pumps run by Angus and Ella MacFadyen. The messages bought, the news of the day exchanged, Danny thoroughly fussed over by everyone present, not least the proprietors, the two of us meandered our way back in the warm sunshine, down the Minister's Brae and past the Power House where the generators had been switched off till teatime to save local electricity bills. The chug-free calm was filled with birdsong, the thinning voices of the robins, the uncertain rehearsals from lingering newly grown willow warblers from that summer season's crop, the chattering on the telephone wires of the families of swallows who would also soon be flying away to Africa and, all along the roadside, the dark green fuchsia bushes were dripping with crimson flowers, bursts of deep colour and intensity on this vividly beautiful late summer day.

We were ready for our lunch on our return, but the lady of the house first calmly fed us news that she was pretty sure the baby was coming, four weeks ahead of schedule. I must have wound the handle on the magneto telephone particularly vigorously as I put through the necessary phone call via Flora at the Exchange, who always asked after Jane, but she could tell something was up and I breathlessly imparted everything she and a soon to be alerted island would want to know. Doctor Andrew

Hall-Gardiner and his wife, Margaret, the District Nurse, were quickly on the scene looking slightly anxious, but fully alive to the prospect of a birth as well as, no doubt, the risks which it was now far too late to mitigate in a mainland hospital.

Preparations were made, important items were urgently transferred from the Doctor's car to the bedroom, water was put on our Calor Gas stove to boil, towels were fetched and mum-to-be-again installed in the marriage bed in which, it had suddenly become clear, there was a major design fault, one which had never even flickered across its young designer's mind. The mattress on the chipboard base supported by kiln bricks gave it a working height of about nine inches above the floorboards, which is clearly less than ideal if you are responsible for delivering a baby and, though Andrew and Margaret made light of it at the time, it wasn't really that much of a surprise when, a few months later, they offered us an old double bed of theirs which they said was surplus to their requirements. We gratefully accepted, for their sake as much as ours.

In all the frantic coming and going I had forgotten only one thing – Danny, where on earth was he? He had chosen his moment to carry out an overdue inspection of the living-room chimney which must have been on his mind for a while and, admittedly, he was the perfect height for the job. Standing tall in the fireplace he had found no problem poking his head right up the lum and, judging by the delight all over his blacked-out face, didn't seem that bothered by the surprisingly large quantity of soot that he had been able to dislodge in the process, mostly over himself, but more than enough to fill the hearth and cover quite a bit of carpet as well. The clean-up process completed, I passed him over to our loving neighbours at Hazel Cottage for safekeeping, a home from home where the ladies of the house, Catriona and her sister Foelallie, could be relied upon to indulge a small person's every last whim except, perhaps, another chimney examination.

Meantime, the baby next door just kept on coming and coming as if there wasn't a moment to lose. As on the previous occasion I took my place at head-end of the bed and began once again to experience the bone-crushing power of the grip of a woman in labour – and though I was in some pain as a result it didn't seem like the moment to mention it. The doctor and nurse knelt at the business end in biblical concentration, the doctor now too preoccupied to take a drag on either one of the two Capstan Full Strength cigarettes he had parked in ashtrays on each side of the bedroom and which, as a committed chain-smoker, he clearly needed and deserved to help him through days like this.

Can I now faithfully recall the finale, when it seemed that time stood still and this unassuming room became the very cen-tre of the universe while a tinier than usual little girl, our Katie, formed from stardust, made her astonishing, early evening arrival on our floor-hugging, homemade bed? I can only really remem-ber feeling the utter magic in the air and seeing it reflected in the faces of everyone else present. All anxieties, personal or shared, evaporated as we basked in the afterglow of the wondrous event we had just witnessed. So quick had been the birth that Danny was retrieved and introduced to his sister, the first baby to have been born on the island for many years, by his normal bedtime. The islanders were so pleased for us and the island of which we were all a part, and they were more than happy to show it in the hours and days to follow. Our wee Katie, who at just four-and-three-quarter pounds I could easily cradle in the cupped palms of my potters' hands, took her place as the newest mem-ber of a sizeable clan of several other island Kates or Katies. She was 'Katie Photter' now, and belonged to the Colonsay family almost as much as she did to her natural one.

Three years and a bit later, in the small hours of a dark and damp December morning, but this time securely within the confines of Oban Maternity Hospital, our Georgie came to join us, flagging up his essential take on life with a great big, humor-ous wink. Home was never better to get back to, and George received the hero's welcome accorded to each and every island baby. His father, who, with a bit too much self-satisfaction, had been accepting the kind words and enquiries of well-wishers as he resumed his island life, was unprepared for the variation on the theme he received the first time he saw Old Peter again. Pressing his face close up to mine so that, with his weak and watery eyesight, he could be sure to savour my reaction, he gave his characteristic sniff and delivered his verdict: 'Ach well, you'll need to tie a knot in it now, Potter!' followed by a well-pleased but uncharacteristic cackle as he took in my reaction. Though it was not possible to follow this injunction to the letter I could see what Peter was getting at and, as it transpired, the fourth and last member of the family, our Robbie, didn't arrive for another ten years, when the story of our lives had moved on. Meantime, we now had three children under five years old and that was, indeed, plenty for both parents to be getting on with.

These days grandchildren help bring back to me what our family life was like: brimful with the chatter and clatter of small people; helpless babies becoming tottering toddlers becoming little children, their daily lives an infinite succession of fresh, existential moments: of drama, adventure, discovery, utter originality, miniscule to major disasters, demands, disappointments, fun, laughter, frustrations, rows, tears, cuddles, mealtimes, snacktimes, story times, nappy times, getting dressed, getting changed, getting undressed, bottles, bathtimes, bedtimes, night-night sleep-tight times and that's only a fraction of it. The lives of the caring adults were subsumed into their children's for just as long as they could stay focused and awake, and even when I wasn't they filled my dreams and featured in occasional night-mares, such as the recurring one I used to have before George was born when Danny and Katie were the size of peas, had somehow fallen through a crack in the floorboards and I was desperately trying to rescue them by weak torchlight. Not good after a long day, as it would invariably wake me up.

It was ordinary, instinctive family life, full of nourishing warmth and uncomplicated love, mostly taken for granted but with occasional moments of realisation which I can re-run in my mind's eye like video clips. Danny in his homemade dungarees, charging across the grass towards the pottery just as fast as his little legs can carry him, shouting that it's lunchtime, it's lunchtime, arms spread out wide in anticipation of his father's embrace. Kate, sitting in the bath with her two brothers, maintaining a continuous flow of chatter about this, that and the other, never forgetting the necessity of instructing the boys firmly as and when required, which was quite often, and then leading the manic and very noisy charge around the armchair that preceded jimjam and story time, an expression of uninhibited *joie de vivre* the like of which I have never since seen bettered. George, who so loved his nappy-changer blowing on his tummy that he added an extra dimension to the normal concept of merriment. 'Again' was almost his very first word. And not forgetting our cat 'Mic-Mac', whose life Reilly would have envied, our productive if ultimately ill-fated little red hens and our two white Aylesbury ducks, who graced the harbour when the tide was in and disgraced themselves by trying to paddle in a pool of tar melted by the sun on one of those heatwave days when Colonsay could have been just another Mediterranean island.

Their parents lived their love for each other through the lives of their beloved children and – most of the time – were not inclined to think that that their own relationship would not continue to take care of itself, subject as it was to what, judging by other couples' lives as well as their own, were the to-be-expected ups and downs. There was so much shared experience and enjoyment in the life that we had, extraordinarily it seemed, come together out of nowhere to make for ourselves and our family in our special island home, that to even question it was as hard as, when one of those inevitable moments came, painful. Though I was hardly aware at the time that I took my new-found life far too much for granted, when I did stop to think it seemed as if I was the luckiest man alive to be raising a wonderful family with such a lovely woman – that was my bottom line and I clung to it with a strong inclination to avoid any further discomforting analysis.

The pain of the misunderstanding moment was never more acute or more public than when I, playfully and really rather amusingly it seemed to me at the time, refused Jane's 'ladies choice' invitation to dance at a ceilidh in the village hall that we had carefully planned to go to together, leaving the children in the loving hands of Foelallie, our trusty babysitter. The totally unexpected and resounding slap Jane gave me for my cleverness left my left ear ringing, both our faces burning and the hall full of stunned witnesses to the incident with a headline story for the late edition of the *Colonsay Gazette*. The evening out together was in ruins and we drove home in the very frostiest of silences to relieve our faithful neighbour before she had barely had time to make her first cup of tea. As usual, the thaw came, things returned to normal and life went on happily – so what was there to worry about? Only time would eventually tell.

For the children the world they encountered beyond the front door was a warm and friendly one where the locals were known and trusted, and if it really did resemble the one since depicted in Mairi Hedderwick's 'Katie Morag' stories, then it must be because there was little to choose between growing up in one small Hebridean island and another. It was an unrushed world where people always had the time and the interest to stop and talk, not least with children, and even when car-bound no one would think of passing an island child or adult by without giving a friendly smile and a wave. It was a world of taken-for-granted island wonders; ferries and fishing boats to observe, beaches to play on, rock-pools to explore, peopled with familiar island characters, pals to exchange visits with, ceilidhs and a full catalogue of other social events to attend. And when the first day of school eventually came there was Charlie McKinnon and his friendly school bus pulling in at the telephone kiosk to provide a VIP welcome to the new passenger. Danny couldn't wait to get on and get into Kilchattan Primary School on the other side of the island, his only stipulation being that he always had a personally brewed flask of tea to take with him. Katie, on the other hand, was outraged by the prospect of having to go to school, refused point-blank to get on the bus and, after separate chauffeur-driven delivery, spent most of her first day curled up asleep under the desk of her understanding teacher, Margaret Walker. Next morning, having slept a bit more on the matter, she couldn't wait to join her friends on the school bus and never looked back.

Their parents too truly loved this island world, but as time went by the first, uncomfortable doubts crept in and kept on returning. Was Colonsay, precious to us as it had become, really the right place for us all to boldly go, live long and prosper? Would there not be more scope for each and all of us to develop in a larger, busier, more 'normal' community, with many more educational, social and economic opportunities than this tiny community could ever offer? Sure, it might, probably would, feel less cosy and intimate to start with, but wasn't that a price worth paying for a new and ultimately more fulfilling life? Life moves on, nothing stays the same, honeymoon periods fade, reality insists on making its presence felt. Yes, but . . . could we really bear to actually leave? We were just joining the long and serpentine column of islanders who had wrestled with these same questions and we wouldn't be the last. It had been said that you only became a true 'local' once you had dug and burnt seven peat stacks in the place, and though old Ross was the only person on the island who still cut peat we were getting very close to metaphorical qualification when the questions started to demand proper answers. Was this the time to be going or to committing ourselves body and soul to the life of this island we now knew and, warts and all, loved so well?

Though we had kept our concerns to ourselves, the topic was about to become the main, the only, talking-point of the whole island. Our neighbour Finlay called in late one evening looking for all the world as if he was going to tell us someone had died. It seemed every bit as bad: his brother Angus, Ella and their four children, 'wee' Angus, the twins Kirsty and Ishbel and Hector, would be selling up and leaving their island home for good to make a new life together on the mainland. Like every other resident we felt the wave of initial shock run through us: this really was news, hard to take news, and brought home the level of interdependence and fragility of our shared existence, the extent to which we lived our individual island lives as members of what amounted to one big, though barely big enough, extended family. If our postie, Big Angus, who with his wife Ella ran the post office and petrol pumps, pedigree islanders both, in their prime, at the very heart of the community's daily round, had decided to call time on living in the very theatre of their generations-deep, family connections and memories, taking their children, who had grown up in the island and who also represented a large slice of the island's youth, with them, then what did it say about the reality and the future of Colonsay life for the rest of us with children to raise, livings to earn and lives to be lived?

Little more than a week before they left the island, BBC Scotland TV's first ever, very late at night, Gaelic current affairs programme, *'Bonn Còmhraidh'* 'Conversation Topic', decided to come to Colonsay and try to get to the heart of the matter. They accompanied Big Angus as he drove his familiar red postbus round Colonsay and over the strand to Oronsay for almost his final delivery. He compared the island of his teenage years in the late 1940s and early fifties when he got his first job at the Home Farm in Kiloran – one of then around thirty Estate employees, an island population of around 250, every house then lived in, more than thirty children in the two-teacher school – with the island of half its population and school-roll size that he was leaving behind nearly thirty years later. By 1978 the core wintertime population had declined to not much more than 100, Estate jobs had been cut to a handful, a dozen houses lay vacant and local children had to leave the island at the age of twelve to get their secondary education on the mainland.

Other island stalwarts chipped in. Big Peter pointed to four island households living in caravans while good homes belonging to the Estate lay empty. Donald Garvard described the challenges and costs involved in running a small hill farm in the Hebrides, the impossibility that crofting alone could ever provide anything like enough income to sustain a household without supplementary sources of income. That, Angus Clark echoed, was the root of the problem: there wasn't enough paid work available on Colonsay, so most islanders had to go the mainland to get jobs with little chance of returning – not that there would be much chance of getting a house to rent off the Estate. Save for Flora Oronsay giving Big Angus her classic Hebridean welcome and invocation to take a cup of tea when he crossed the threshold of Oronsay farmhouse with the mails, there were no female voices to be heard in this otherwise authentic and, for a rarity, public commentary by Colonsay's native Gaels on their island's socio-economic problems and seemingly relentless decline; all of which I had heard and discussed countless times with my regular visitors to the pottery.

The two very English voices given airtime sounded out of place and unconvincing in the otherwise undiluted Colonsay Gaelic context of the programme. First, the laird, Lord Strathcona, replied to the question of what he was doing for the island by pointing out that he was providing capital and revenue and, he 'liked to think, leadership'. 'Why so many empty houses then?' elicited the unexpected response, 'Touché'. Secondly, at a public meeting convened at short notice by the Highlands and Islands Development Board to show willing, if not entirely able, and which the native islanders felt could also be doing a lot more for the island, up piped the potter with the suggestion that all holiday homes on the island should be taxed and the money put towards reducing the cost per unit of electricity from the island price of 15p to the mainland norm of 3p. It seemed like a perfectly reasonable idea at the time.

The programme came to its conclusion with Big Angus singing at a ceilidh in the Village Hall, making yet another one of his inimitable contributions to island life that we would soon all have to get used to living without. He sang the popular Gaelic love song, '*Far an robh mi n'raoir*' ('Where I was yesterday') as beautifully as he had ever done, and the chorus line had an extra poignancy, given where his and his family's yesterday would soon be as they embraced their new tomorrow. It was a picture that seemed to encapsulate the pathos of Gaelic-speaking islanders, whose older-fashioned culture and take on life, once protected by its over-the-horizon isolation from mainland and mainstream customs, were no longer strong or remote enough to withstand the irresistible attractions and pressures exerted by the big, brash and unstoppable modern world.

I could not say that the exodus of the post office branch of the MacFadyens was the point where I turned my head, though not my heart, away from Colonsay. After Andrew Oronsay, the peerless piper, had played his own heart out on the pierhead for the departing family, the tears of the huge island turnout been shed and eyes dried, island life flipped surprisingly quickly and unsentimentally back to business more or less as usual, and I needed to get some more pots fired, as Easter was less than a week away and the first of the season's visitors would be making their welcome return. Why would we want to leave anyway? Our lives were deeply intertwined in the life of the island on top of our own, full-on family life. The children were happily immersed in their pre-school, primary school and out-of-school activities, and their parents took active parts in just about every single community organisation and organised event going, from the long-established ones like the Women's Guild and WRI to the new kids on the block, the Colonsay Electricity Company and the Community Council. Then there were all the private ploys designed to keep amusement levels topped up, now including trips in the twenty-four-foot launch driven by an ancient Kelvin 'Poppet' – a name to suit its noise – petrol/paraffin engine, which I had not long acquired from old Dan McKechnie, former ferryman in the Ross of Mull, and now used for trips with family and friends and other adventures. Was all this not good enough for us?

Not for the young man whose insecurities, though much assuaged by the healing power of a deeply nourishing family and community life, would not let him be satisfied with what he had now grown used to and took too much for granted; insecurities for which he always seemed to be able to find scapegoats. Nor for his wife, who was also looking for more prospects than life in this tiny island community seemed able to offer, more for the children, more for the grown-ups, more for the whole family.

Our eventual decision to leave Colonsay came opportunistically. In the late 1970s the HIDB were encouraging communities to set up co-operatives to develop community-owned and controlled projects which the Board and the communities concerned believed would bring them much-needed economic and social benefits. If the HIDB agreed with the community's business plan then they said that they would give the duly formed co-operative (called a *'co-chomunn'* in Gaelic-speaking areas) a grant, provided it was matched pound for pound by money raised through a share purchase by as many members of the community as possible. Shares normally cost £50 each. I liked the thinking behind this really innovative community development approach, which I thought could just have worked in Colonsay had the population been a bit bigger and generally better able to invest all the extra effort and willpower, never mind the cash, that would be involved in trying to identify and then get going realistically viable projects in an island where they would almost certainly face the extra challenge of getting the Estate to give its wholehearted support, project by project. It seemed like an ambition too far in that era.

The Uists are a group of islands, with causeway interconnections, which form the middle section of the Outer Hebrides. Although they lie even further out in the Atlantic than Colonsay, they are in comparison full of people and life, and the population of the Uists alone was then in excess of five thousand, the overwhelming majority of whom were native Gaelic speakers. Under the leadership of a very remarkable local priest, Father Colin McInnes, the district of Iochdar at the northern end of the island of South Uist had just set up their own community co-op, *Co-chomunn an Iochdar*, and were looking for their first manager. After long discussions in Glen Cottage after the children had been tucked up, we agreed that I should throw my hat into the ring. We were both ready, so we thought, to move on from our Colonsay life to what should be a more fulfilling but still island life in the Uists. Once again, it seemed like a perfectly reasonable idea at the time.

I got the job and, even though alarm bells started ringing as we waited and waited in months-long limbo for Father Colin to secure the house he had promised to find for us, the day we had all been dreading eventually came, when the Alexander family had to make their own tearful farewells on the pier and climb up the gangway to join the long line of Colonsay emigrants who had gone before them. We too were piped onto the ferry, but we were quite unprepared for the 'emigrants' wave' goodbye after the ferry had cast off. Long after the faces and waving hands of our fellow islanders on the end of the pier had become indistinguishable, we could see white bedsheets being waved by our friends and erstwhile neighbours outside their respective homes or, more accurately, by the ladies of those houses with whom we had previously made our farewells on the grounds that they couldn't face doing so on the pier: amongst them our next-door neighbours and faithful babysitters, Catriona and Foelallie, Mary Clark outside her home higher up the hill, Maggie MacAllister next door to the shop, and round the shore in Glassard, Jasper Brown's wife Katie 'Cholla', Big Peter's wife Mary Ann MacAllister, and further along the street Old Katie MacAllister and her neighbour Flora Oronsay, who had recently retired there from Oronsay Farm with husband Andrew.

The waving bedsheets themselves soon became distant specks on the rapidly disappearing island but, truth to tell, we had been unable to see them clearly for some time before that as our tears flowed and our hearts broke. What on earth were we doing? More to the personal point, what was I doing for my family and why had I really done it? It wouldn't take very long to find out, but that is another story.

For Katie Photter on her 40th birthday

I remember, I remember – it seems like yesterday,
A day in sweet September on an island far away,
The sunshine of late summer but with autumn in the air
And the hedgerows dripping fuchsia, crimson fuschia,
　　everywhere.

In a cottage by a harbour, a whitewashed but-and-ben,
Lived a potter and his lover and their small red-headed
son.
The potter was a bearded scruff whose feet were made
of clay
And the lady was so lovely that she took your breath away.

She was carrying a baby that was waiting to be born
But in a mainland hospital the Doctor had forsworn.
No need to catch the ferry yet, the birth was weeks away,
Of that we were quite certain on that soft September day.

But the baby had no notion – strange though it seems
today –
Of the concept of *mañana* or even some delay,
For on that Monday morning, with the washing out to
dry,
The baby thought 'I'm ready, and if you're not, don't ask
why.'

The Doctor soon was summoned and his wife the District
Nurse
And both looked rather anxious at this masterplan reverse.
By habit a chain-smoker of the full-strength cigarette,
The Doctor inhaled deeply and then broke out in a sweat.

Soon all was hustle-bustle as Plan B sprang into action,
But 'where was our wee Danny?' the sudden thought had
come.
He had seized the perfect moment of contraction-led
distraction
And was busy in the fireplace with his head stuck up the
lum.

Our good Hebridean neighbours came quickly to the
rescue

And the little boy was gathered up and gently whisked
   next door,
While in the whitewashed cottage the baby kept on
   coming –
A tiny girl had come to join us and be loved for evermore.

And the room was filled with magic as you lay there in
   your newness,
A speck upon the marriage bed that gave our hearts such
   thrill,
And your you-ness was so special that we might have
   called you Eunice,
But luckily we named you Kate and our Kate-o you are
   still.

Now forty years like forty birds into the heavens have
   flown,
And you're a woman in her prime with children of your
   own,
A loving man, a lovely home, a family full of love,
A life that's rich with blessings and I thank the stars above.

I remember, I remember, it seems like yesterday,
A day in sweet September, Scalasaig on Colonsay,
The sunshine of late summer but with autumn in the air
And the hedgerows dripping fuchsia, crimson fuschia,
   everywhere.

15

LASTING IMPRESSIONS

Unlike those shiploads of eighteenth and nineteenth-century emigrants who had to make their island farewells believing that they would never set eyes on Colonsay again, we were able to keep in frequent touch through letters, long phone calls and fairly regular holidays. Though as the chapters of our family life unfolded, the island's siren call became less insistent, it never went away; and if nowadays I don't get to step ashore there as often as I would like, I still go back there time and time again in the merest blink of my inner eye.

And when I daydream about my favourite corner of the island landscape and seascape, I can all but taste the air and feel the ground beneath my feet again as I wend my imaginary way across the airstrip and southernmost portion of the golf course on my familiar route to Ardskenish; jinking over the stones in *ath nan corp*, 'the ford of the bodies', where the track crosses the burn that runs into the long sandy bay of *port lobh*, the aptly-named 'smelly seaweed harbour'; watching the rabbits scuttle down their holes as I follow the green-grassed track up the last corner of the *machaire beag*, 'the wee machair', musing as ever on all the pre-emigration families that once populated just this one small corner of modern day Machrins Farm, long since deserted save for the faint traces of their former homes; on through the crumbling stone pillars known as *geata druim shligeach*, 'shelly ridge gate', skirting the deep ruts as the track becomes muddy, then snakes its way upward through *turnigil*, 'twisting gully', to *druim reidh*, 'smooth ridge', where, now full of anticipation as I hear the sound of the sea beyond, I drop down through the rocky pass, *bealach na traigh*, 'the pass of the bay', where old Ross left his marker stone and where, once again, I am brought to a standstill by the sight of the Ardskenish panorama spread out before me like a banquet prepared for an emperor.

If some of the topographical details are getting a bit blurred at the edges then I know that I can always check them out again when next I'm over. Not so, though, the cast list of characters who once filled my island world, now all but gone, save in the memory where they still strut their stuff when called upon to do so or, better still, when they just slip back into consciousness, unbeckoned but always welcome, to deliver some touchstone reminder and, almost invariably, the inner chuckle that goes with it. Those leading lights of yesteryear may have quit centre stage, but not without leaving lasting impressions on those who were lucky enough to experience them in both regular and, not infrequently, epic flow.

Those that I got to know best while I played my own bit part were mostly near neighbours and regular callers at the pottery. None more welcome than the Darroch brothers, Neil and Ross, who lived next door to each other in their semi-detached bungalows on Scalasaig's *srathaid chaim*, 'Squint Street', and only a few paces away from 'Maggie Thomson's cottage', after their Orcadian mother's maiden name, the home in which they were born and raised before and during the First World War. Their Darroch surname – the Gaelic word for 'oak' – was about right, because they had to become that tough from an early age, not just to get by on the basics in the very money-poor island community of those times, but to survive childhood diphtheria when the medicine proffered to them in their sick beds, they would recall, was a teaspoonful of whisky. From an early age they doubled as the men of the house since their father, Alasdair, worked much of his life at sea, so they only saw him if he managed to get home 'between boats' or on his fortnight's annual leave, when he returned to cut the peats. The boys left school aged fourteen just as the world was entering the great post-war depression and, with paying work hard to find either on Colonsay or the mainland, they decided in their early twenties that they would try their luck in Canada, taking their special attributes – not least their hardiness – with them.

There they discovered that life was even tougher in the New World than it was in the Old, but they were young and resilient and they worked their way from city to city and farm to farm, 'riding the rails' like so many other young men from so many other corners of Europe and North America on similar survival missions during those hard times. They hitched free lifts on passing freight trains as the prospect or even the rumour of a few days' work dictated; sometimes, they would tell me, walking the railtrack for miles and miles without food when they had jumped from a train only to find that their luck had run out and a rumoured job had already been snatched up by another of the many similar competitors. They lived their Canadian adventure for several years, but as the Great Depression deepened they decided to come back home to Colonsay where they made livelihoods for themselves fishing lobsters along the west coast from May till October and snaring rabbits on Oronsay in the winter – their best haul being 3,700 pairs caught between November and early April when, with the first of the spring lambs becoming due, they would carefully gather up and pack away all their snares and turn their attention again to getting the boat scraped and painted and the creels repaired in preparation for the coming season of lobster fishing. They were skilled, hard-grafting islanders who could turn their hand to most tasks on land or sea and, when they had some time available, were also much in demand from island farmers.

They had not long reached pensionable age – younger than I am today – when I first got to know them and were still very active, intelligent and observant, their faces lined with character. Both smoked the occasional pipe and practised all the mesmerising rituals that went with that once familiar art, bringing a smoke-curling and occasionally eye-watering atmosphere to the stories and reflections that they loved to share.

Neil was the more compact of the two, shoulders somewhat stooped by a lifetime of heavy lifting, or so it seemed, though still as strong as an ox. I once came across him walking home-ward shouldering an oversized section of a tree, still complete with branches, which had got blown down by a gale in a patch of woodland known as 'the glebe', and was ripe for foraging. He and his future firewood were the very apparition of a tree with legs, and so filled the width of the single-track road that it was much like encountering a section of Birnam Wood making its Shakespearian journey to Dunsinane. When I pulled the car into the passing place to give him and his tree room to pass, though not without offering to give him a hand, he engaged me in unhurried conversation about this, that and the other, apparently quite oblivious of his burden. What's more, he didn't even bother to put it down before, an unconscionable time later so it seemed to me, politely declining my repeated offer and pro-ceeding on his journey – and he was still half a mile from home – leaving me feeling like an even bigger heel than Macbeth.

Ross was the taller; looser-limbed with long strong arms and large, expressive hands, which flitted like monstrous butterflies within conversational sight-lines as he re-told and often re-en-acted a favourite story plus, for extra emphasis though it was hardly required, waving his great forefinger and gnarled thumb in the air like a Colt 45 with the hammer fully cocked, his other three impressive digits playing support roles. Outdoors he wore a fisherman's cap, dark blue and with a shiny peak, donated and renewed every few years by his cousin – and my neighbour – Finlay, whose uniform allowance from his part-time job look-ing after Colonsay's small lighthouse for the Northern Light-house Board was sufficient to keep them both in their favoured bonnets.

Neil, on the other hand, preferred a grey, flat cap with a popper on its peak, which might occasionally be unpopped in extreme weather conditions. Like most other male islanders, the brothers' bespoke tailor was the Islay Farmers Store, where from time to time they would ask its custodian, Foelallie, to unlock the shed doors so that they could have a rake through the assorted cardboard boxes and find the blue denim jackets and overalls which formed the basic uniform of most Colonsay men and which, along with the donkey jackets, waterproof leggings and wellies, set the workaday sartorial standard. It was always a bit disconcerting, nevertheless, to see some familiar figure sporting a newly purchased item before its colour and design had been moulded by repeated use into the usual body shape and the true character of its owner.

Though next-door neighbours and close brothers, they led largely independent lives; Neil the more home-loving and inclined to contemplative consideration of life's inexhaustible curiosities, though always ready to share the fruits of his carefully considered cogitations. Ross was the keener to get out of the house to exercise his remarkable skills at living off the land, and would often call by the pottery on his way out towards the lighthouse on the *rudha dubh,* 'dark point', from where, armed only with a length of plain fencing wire, he would stride back an hour or two later with a rabbit or two for the pot. He knew the rough ground like the back of one his hardworking hands, and knew too that, rather than running all the way back to a more distant hole, a startled rabbit would often take quick shelter under a convenient boulder. Knowing every angle in every rock as he did, Ross also knew when and where he would be able to insert his wire, twist it gently but firmly into the fur of the rabbit and patiently ease it out of its hiding place for instant despatch. If he fancied a goose, duck or lobster on his menu, then he would make his way on his well-used pushbike down to either the Machrins or the Garvard route to Ardskenish.

If Garvard, then, after stopping at the farm to share tea and gather intelligence from Donald Garvard on the latest comings and goings in the local bird world, he would walk out with borrowed shotgun across *Traigh nam Barc,* 'beach of the breaking waves', to his happy hunting grounds. He would never return empty-handed, but with the catch of the day plus extras like a piece of decent rope gathered from the shore or, if in season, some peewits or seagulls eggs as well. So adept was Ross at satisfying his material needs with very little, that when he decided a few years later to make life a bit easier on himself by replacing his pushbike with a spanking new moped, he was able to save enough from his state pension, his one and only source of cash income, to effect the purchase within a remarkably small number of months, his biggest financial sacrifice being to sign a pledge to himself not to go the pub for the duration – a pledge from which he never once wavered.

Ross summed up his philosophy of life for me one time I was visiting by rummaging through a pile of back issues of an assortment of old magazines that filled a corner of his living room like a snowdrift. Eventually he laid his great hands on a well-thumbed copy of the *Scots Magazine* and opened it up at an article about travelling people in the west of Scotland with a quote from one of the travellers, 'If I can't be free to choose to live my life the way I want, then what is the purpose of living?'. He laid the magazine on my lap and stabbed the crucial paragraph with one of his huge digits, and the only other verbal explanation he chose to offer was 'Ach, ya know what I mean!'

Each brother would call by as he made his way to the shop and to see what was doing at the harbour and, during the summer and autumn, to check their rowing boat moored inside the breakwater on the far side and which they would take out, often together, to catch saithe, mackerel and the occasional big lithe. On one occasion while working away quietly in the pottery I was roused from my concentration by a frantic shout from Neil, which suggested he might have fallen into the harbour after returning from one of his fishing trips. It was worse than that: absorbed in gutting his freshly caught fish on the rocks he had failed to notice that the tide had crept in just enough to float his untied boat which he had parked temporarily on the dried-out harbour bottom because he couldn't yet reach his mooring. He'd forgotten to secure it, though, and as the tide began to fill the harbour again an offshore breeze had sprung up and was now blowing the brothers' pride and joy slowly but surely out towards the open sea. We both took off at the same time to make a dash round the harbour in the hope of catching the boat as it slid past the harbour steps, the younger man with a good head start. Half way there, Neil, not normally the shouting type, gave vent to another anguished bellow as, to add insult to injury, he saw that a gaggle of seagulls had now discovered his partially gutted catch where the drifting boat crisis had forced him to abandon it. Out of a clear blue sky his successful fishing trip had suddenly turned into a nightmare, and I have an abiding if fleeting image of Neil, stranded equidistantly between the two unfolding disasters, just too far away from each to do anything to stop either, and giving a perfect impression of a man whose every mental fuse was blowing at the same time while he tried to figure out which way he should turn – a feeling which I have more than once since shared. I managed to catch the boat and Neil retrieved enough remaining fish from his pillaged catch to make a meal when he got home, and we were both able to dine out on the story his misadventure had given us.

Both men had fertile minds, particularly where some creative recycling was involved. On these grounds alone Neil hated throwing anything away, no matter how far gone the article might appear to others. He saw a late flowering opportunity for a pair of old wellies by cutting the tops off them carefully so that he could slip off his house slippers and use the welly bottoms, worn smooth by use but still waterproof, as quick slip-ons when he needed to pop across the wet terrain at his back door to refill his coal bucket. He could not, though, bring himself to discard the tops and was deeply satisfied when, a couple of years later, inspiration came upon him as to their redeployment. Neil simply detested the draughts in his house and had been long engaged fighting a battle of wills with them. His resistance efforts included laying miles and miles of draught-proofing defences, notwithstanding which he just couldn't seem to block out the one that nipped the back of his heels when he was sitting at his fireside watching the telly. So it was that when, one cold and windy winter's evening, I called to visit him for my Gaelic lesson I noticed that he was wearing something green and distinctly odd-looking over the bottom of his trouser legs

– those sawn-off welly tops which now fitted snugly over the tops of his house slippers! The guerrilla draught had finally been outmanoeuvred and Neil wore the well-pleased look of a man whose heels would never be draught-nipped again, and whose waste-not want-not credo had been triumphantly vindicated.

If anything Ross was an even more inventive recycler and, on one of my winter evening visits to Squint Street, he beckoned me next door to show me his latest recycling creations – some highly imaginative creel designs which fully deserved to be patented, including one made out of an old plastic milk crate and the other from a length of enticingly – for a lobster – open-ended clay drainage pipe, which now had a kind of trap door at one end held open by a strong elastic band. As the lobster, he explained, made its way inside the pipe towards the lure of the bait it would discover, too late, that it had not only sprung the trap door firmly behind, but was now held at its front end by an extra strong rabbit snare made out of brass wire.

Ross was locally renowned for his habitual use of creative catchphrases, foremost of which, in response to normal enquiries about his well-being was 'Mighty fine!' usually followed by 'Never died a winter yet!' but they also included originals like 'When men were men and women were double-breasted', to describe the good old days, which for extra emphasis would be finished off with his favourite stand-by of all, 'Ach, ya know what I mean!' accompanied by a characteristic flit or two of the big right hand in Colt 45 mode. He had other nuggets too which he saved for special, storytelling occasions, such as 'He didn't know his airse from a hole in the ground . . . ya know what I mean!' or 'A motley crew from the good ship Kangaroo . . .' usually introduced to illustrate sightings of unfamiliar visitors coming ashore from a passing yacht. He would come away with freshly minted one-liners too which brightened everyone's day, even if you were at the receiving end, as when he passed public comment on my lying ill in bed with the mumps: 'The Potter's got myxomatosis!', and given that the big butterfly hand was flitting around crotch level it hardly merited the addition of 'ya know what I mean!'.

To top it all, Ross had a well-loved store of stanzas from his favourite poet, Robert Service, 'the bard of the Yukon', which he was wont to share when in convivial mood and company: 'A bunch of the boys were whooping it up . . .', 'There are strange things done in the midnight sun . . .' and 'Boys, says he, ya don't know me and none of you give a damn , . .' being amongst his favourites; and if he was in the right mood then you might be lucky enough to hear his inimitable recital of a full stanza or more.

Although, more often than not, I encountered them singly, I think of them now not just together but along with the remaining member of the combined Darroch ménage of that time – Jim, pronounced 'Jum', Ross's small, shrewd and universally popular black and brown dog, who went with him everywhere, whether on foot to the shop or pub or, if further afield, riding in the front basket of the moped. 'Jum! Be a flat dog!', was his master's singular command when in company, and Jim would lie down at Ross's feet like the best of dogs that he was, though he kept ears and usually one eye open so as not to miss anything. I picture the three as I came across them when I called at Neil's one winter's evening, the men of oak weak with laughter and Jim barking and wagging his tail in companionable solidarity. They had been enjoying their bachelors' privileges of replacing the front forks on Neil's upside-down bike in front of his living room fire and, having carefully re-fitted the handlebars, front wheel and brakes, were sitting back contemplating yet another job well done – until one of them noticed that they had somehow put everything back together back to front and now had a strangely inverted bike with the front wheel where the handlebars should be and vice versa although, in the upside down position the bicycle otherwise still looked disconcertingly convincing. To them it was just one more example to add to their lifetime's list of the best-laid plans of mortal man going pear-shaped, and they were relishing the surreal proof of the dictum that they, unwittingly, had painstakingly re-assembled. It did not take them long to put it right though, as Jim and I could have testified once we got our breath back.

Then there were the two Peters MacAllister, fishermen both, nephew and uncle, 'Big' and 'Old'. The pottery became the destination for Old Peter's daily constitutional from his home by the shop where he lived with his older sister, Maggie. When he appeared at the pottery door I would always enquire how he was today and he would normally reply with an 'Ach, I'm no bad,' usually gentle and wistful in tone, occasionally slightly querulous as if to say 'you asked me the same blooming question yesterday'. But sometimes the response was 'Ach, I'm no feeling very great today,' and on one such occasion when I asked if he'd been to see the doctor he responded with his trademark sniff that he had, but that he might just as well not have bothered: 'He gave me some pills no bigger than a pin's head,' (pause for another, equally contemptuous sniff), 'you'd be better eating cow's shite!' It was the paltry size of the proffered remedy that had moved him to spit out such a scathing pharmaceutical review, though it was clear that the patient was much improved by the telling of the story, as was the potter by yet another example of the humour and timing that flowed so effortlessly from Hebridean lips, and where even an exceptional vulgarity was transformed by the soft and musical inflections that native Gaelic-speakers would bring to bear on the expression and articulation of their second language.

Old Peter, or *Para Clocs,* as for reasons I never discovered he was also commonly known, was a ship's carpenter to trade who had worked for years in the great shipyards of the Clyde during its early twentieth-century heyday, but the stories and memories he preferred to share were mainly from his formative island years, growing up in the fishing village of Riasg Buidhe in which he was born in 1900. I was fascinated by these keyhole glimpses that my time-travelling visitors would give me of this pre-First World War Colonsay, which they had been part of and could still see so vividly in their minds' eyes. I wished I could do too and, given half a chance by the storyteller, would probe them for more as if, by sheer enthusiasm, I would one day unlock the door and finally enter this private world of theirs, which somehow seemed so much truer and fuller of meaning than my own.

'Do you remember the Professor at all, Peter?' I once asked him during a pipe-lighting intermission in the conversational flow.

'Ach aye, I remember him fine. He was a nice old man – a great friend of my father's. *Domhnull Miogaras* ['Donald from Miogaras'] they called him. That's the bit behind the school and Baptist church, there used to be a wee bit croft there that his father got – his father was from Mull.'

'From Mull, Peter, I never knew that?'

'Aye, he was a McKinnon from Mull but he married a Colonsay woman, a Currie, and that was where the Professor was born.'

'He was born in 1839, Peter – I've just been reading some of his stuff.'

'Ach well, that's where he was born, anyway, Miogaras. They stayed up in the farmhouse at Balnahard for years and he kept his boat, the *Seasgair* she was called – I remember her fine – a skiff, and he used to keep her moored in *Poll na Cnarradh* ['The pool of the vessel'] behind *Sgeir nic Fhionnlaidh* ['Finlay's daughter's skerry'] at the far end yonder of Balnahard Bay. My father used to help the Professor look after her when he was away in Edinburgh. He died on Christmas Day the year the First World War started: I remember the funeral fine. Ach aye, he was a nice old man, the Professor – a great friend of my father's.'

'No man is an island', John Donne said, though he would surely have reconsidered had he met Big Peter, *Para Mor,* who seemed to embody the distilled essence of what made Colonsay so special: its very spot in the wide Atlantic ocean, its life story, its native culture and people, its unique character and characters, its particular island humour and way of life. Whether visitor or native, the first person you looked out for and the last you set eyes upon as you drew into or away from the pier on those CalMac transitions from one world to the other was Big Peter. In his yellow oilskins or blue dungarees, standing four-square at the head of the pier whatever the weather, Peter's profile was as unmistakeable as it was reassuring, the close-up view of his windswept forehead, twinkling eyes and, as the years went by, gradually greying beard even more so.

His Colonsay credentials were impeccable: a Buie on his mother's side and a MacAllister on his father's. The Buies were noted oral tradition-bearers, gladly rehearsing and keeping alive the memories and traditional stories of Colonsay people from times gone by. The MacAllisters were consummate raconteurs too, but as seafarers also perhaps more inclined to bring 'off-shore' perspectives to bear on island or any other matters. In any event, Big Peter's contemplative view of the world had been greatly expanded by his many years spent working 'deep sea' as a sailor and boatswain in the merchant marine. He had seen and savoured it for real, and had plenty of voyage time to think about the comparative pros and cons of the island life he had left behind. In the end, it was no contest, he came gratefully home, married his sweetheart, Mary Ann McGilvray, and settled back into the very heart of Colonsay life, looking after his growing family, creeling for lobsters along the island's wild and wave-swept fringes and was employed as GPO engineer and CalMac pierhand when back on dry land.

Peter himself would never have entertained the suggestion that he played such an influential role in the daily life and lives of the island but so he did, quite naturally and almost accidentally. He couldn't help it if he found himself on show on the pier or tucked into his favourite corner of the bar by the door after he had called in for a pre- or post-prandial pint. He couldn't help it either that he had such a keen mind, such a genuine interest in the life-experiences of any other human beings. Islander or visitor, peer of the realm, passer-by or potter, he engaged eas-ily and naturally with anyone and everyone: he enjoyed people without prejudice, and his inviting way of sharing intelligent and humorous conversation, insights and stories was his for the spontaneous giving and yours simply for the taking. Whether new face or familiar old one, he always had time for you.

Conversation was Peter's forte and perfected art form; interesting, stimulating, often astonishingly eclectic, full of Chaucerian diversions and unlikely illustrations – ranging far, wide and effortlessly from, say, discussion arising from a political issue of the moment, a comparison with the approach taken in some exotic and faraway country he had visited, a small diversion while he recalled how he and fellow seaman, 'Happy Jack' from Eriskay, had got arrested and thrown into jail while on shore leave in its capital city through not much fault of their own, he suggested with a chuckle, save for a late-night, cultural misunderstanding; how the First Mate of their ship who had got them released happened to be related through marriage to a second cousin of his mother's who lived in Glasgow, leading back by a route full of circuitous conversational detours to, perhaps, an analysis of the inconsistencies in the forthcoming increases in CalMac freight charges, the implications of the morning's shipping forecast and an assessment on the degree of probability as to whether the ferry would sail tomorrow morning with spare parts for the generator, plus the Estate factor who was coming over to make his promised house visits to discuss a proposed rise in rents.

Though a wonderful talker who would keep his audience by turns informed, amused, provoked, occasionally scandalised but always entertained for sometimes hours on end if time and circumstances favoured, Big Peter was also a keen listener and observer who missed little of importance that was either said or left unsaid. For the younger men of the place, myself included, he provided an unofficial mentoring service based on a shrewd but tolerant understanding of our character traits, particularly those that needed working on. Imparting most of his wisdom tangentially in one-to-one blethers, Peter wouldn't hesitate to bring you back to earth with a salutary bump if you were getting a bit too carried away with yourself for your own good. A humour-laced reality check was generally all it took, not infrequently shared with other appreciative mentees during one of our spontaneous pub tutorials.

He kept us right and, in truth, most of the rest of the island as well. His was the view you – and most other people – sought to compare your own with, the company you would seek to be informed, educated and entertained by, without fail but not in any particular order. There was a calm and consistent rhythm to his approach to life which seemed to exert a gravitational pull and steadying influence on the rest of us. He was pretty well unflappable, and even when tested to the limit would rarely do more than give a sniff before falling into contemplative silence and giving the cause of the offence a withering but somehow forgiving, 'I've seen it all before', look.

Such was the case when I was crewing for Peter on the *Thrive* and responsible for driving the boat to make his creel-lifting task easier. I found, to my horror, that the gear lever had sheared off in my hand as I rammed her into reverse to stop us getting blown onto the rocks in choppy seas. I shouted to Peter but he couldn't hear me over the wind, so I waved the broken bit of lever at him in an explanatory, albeit totally gormless, fashion, as it was now impossible to get the engine out of gear or into another one. I got a long-suffering look in return which lives with me yet as, without a word, he moved swiftly and surefoot-edly from deck to cockpit, opened up his ever-present toolbox, attached a large 'shifter' to the amputated gear stub, advised me in Gaelic what to do with it henceforth *'Gabh e do shocair, a Photter'* ('Take it easy, o Potter') and returned as easily as he came to his creel-lifting station. It had been a nasty moment, but where my imagination had instantly gone into overdrive and had us abandoning ship and clinging to a reef in forlorn hope of a rescue, he gave no sign, other than that fleeting look, that his equanimity had even momentarily been dented. All was customary good humour as we took the short cut back to har-bour through the tide-filled Strand, but I knew there had to be some price to pay for my misdemeanour: nothing worse – or better – than becoming the lead story in the *Colonsay Gazette* that evening as Peter responded with a twinkle in his eye to the usual raft of enquiries about how the fishing had gone that day.

He had, after all, a good story to tell, plenty of time to tell it and always, always an appreciative audience

It looked as if Big Peter was operating a franchise on time itself. Even by generous Hebridean standards, he seemed to have more available than the rest of us, though perhaps it was the way he had of sharing it so limitlessly that gave that impression, because he always found the time to fulfil his many and varied daily commitments. How often, though, did I, like so many, not just bask in the bubbles of conversational timelessness in which Peter would envelop you as he shared views and stories, but also feel a bit left out if I came across him sharing an obviously enjoyable bubble with others which, in my carelessness, I had somehow managed to miss. There he would be in one or other of his familiar dialoguing modes: sitting in his vehicle – the car having supplanted the succession of vans as his family grew – having a one-to-one blether with a passenger or, more often than not, window down and talking to whoever stood outside; or, if out in the open himself, then hands in dungaree or donkey-jacket pockets, leaning into a leeward wall having what looked like a kind of parallel chat with someone, usually similarly dressed, but both heads looking outwards rather than at each other to make sure that no passing event went unremarked. Peter was not a smoker, but during the autumn months he kept pockets full of hazel nuts which he gathered from roadside trees, and Sherlock Holmes would have had little trouble picking up his trail from the cairn-like accumulations of broken shells he left behind him when he moved on from one conversation to another on his daily round. It was neighbourly, it was necessary and there always was and always would be time for the sheer pleasure of a restorative as well as an always informative blether with Big Peter/*Para Mor.*

Or so we all thought until he was taken from us in his prime, suddenly and totally unpreparedly, one unwelcome March morning in 1990. If Colonsay was rocked to its foundations, then the shockwave which followed was felt every bit as hard by his now bereft battalion of friends and followers just wherever they happened to find themselves when the news hit them. Without so much as a by-your-leave, Peter had now absented himself for ever from his pivotal role as the living, breathing and constantly interacting centre of everyday Colonsay life. He now assumed the role of priceless Colonsay touchstone, a henceforth internalised, though still eminently shareable, 'I wonder what Para would have made of it' point of reference and reflection, where fresh and reliable bearings could be sought on matters both Colonsay and personal, though you may or may not be surprised to pick up his familiar chuckle when you do so.

Every community has its local favourites and heroes, some universally acknowledged like Big Peter, but others who receive less of the limelight and are only fully appreciated by smaller but no less devoted audiences. Colonsay has produced a generous share of both and, of whichever variety, they bind people together in a network of friendships and dependencies that bring reality to the notional theory contained in the word 'community'. My personal 'binders' included not only the Darroch brothers, the two Peters and my next door neighbours at Hazel Cottage, but many others I tended to see less of who gave me exactly the same sense of community, the uniquely Colonsay community, to which I then so much needed to belong.

None more so than Donald Garvard: farmer, crofter, bard, piper, singer, occasional actor and master of ceremonies, perceptive, morale-boosting friend and enemy to none, except, in extremis, himself. I see him, slowly and contentedly bestriding his croft at Druim Clach, utterly at home with himself in this matchless slice of Hebridean landscape, his collie dogs and his ewes and his new lambs around him, the baseball cap atop his tonsured head and T-shirt tucked into baggy blue jeans held up by a length of baler twine only adding to the impression that somehow this Gaelic-speaking islander had not long retired from a career coaching the New York Yankees, albeit with midriff now rather more to the fore than it had been in his sporting prime. The same Donald who, on returning to the island after several months away in what was then locally, though not with intentional cruelty, referred to as the 'spin-drier', because more than one islander had had to make the same difficult journey, not only brought his true and wonderful old self back with him but a story which exemplified the magic and the measure of the man.

Part of the treatment included occasional group-therapy sessions where individual patients were encouraged to share their life stories, not only with fellow patients but the doctors and nurses as well. The sessions took place over a morning and afternoon, during which the lives and stories of all the patients would be shared and considered. Donald's was the last name on the list, but the session ended without him being called so it was agreed that they would all reconvene first thing the next morning, so that Donald could have his due turn, the doctor in charge's assumption being that it could all be wrapped up fairly quickly. This was something of a miscalculation, for when Donald started to recount his, by most people's standards, very different kind of upbringing on the farm and island of Oronsay before the Second World War, he did so, it could be deduced, in that characteristically evocative and spellbinding way which only the most gifted of Hebridean storytellers can achieve, and had only got up to his life aged twelve when the group decided, reluctantly, to break for lunch. Moreover, the word quickly went round to everyone in the building who hadn't been there in the morning not on any account to miss the afternoon session, on the grounds that it was absolutely guaranteed to provide unbeatable therapy for all concerned.

Stories within stories within stories are part of the storytelling Gael's recipe, and it is not impossible that in his recollections Donald may have included a favourite Colonsay story, one that was still told by the older islanders who visited my pottery. It featured a mysterious regiment which had once been observed by two men out hunting rabbits by the light of a full moon – another still practised pastime, though the headlight and the spotlight have long since supplanted reliance on moonlight and rubbing the barrels with a little butter beforehand to improve the sighting. The story was always referred to as *Reisemaid Eoghann a Ghlinne*, 'Hugh of the Glen's Regiment', because the principal eye witness was Hugh, a real person, who lived out his early nineteenth-century life in the green and secluded valley called *Gleann Ardinnis*, 'Ardskenish Glen', which lies at the head of the long sandy bay, *Traigh nam Barc*, that separates Garvard Farm from the Ardskenish peninsula.

The story went that Hugh, a man it was always added of unquestionable integrity, and his nameless companion had crept up behind two small hillocks called the *Sithean Mor* and the *Sithean Meadhonach*, 'The big and middle fairy knolls', which lie not far from the head of the bay, and when they peeked carefully over the top looking for undisturbed rabbits to shoot they saw instead an unending file of people, soldiers they presumed, marching three abreast along the track that once ran from the Strand past the bay and through the hilly ground towards distant *Port Lobh* and the *Machaire Beag*. They estimated that the human file must have stretched all the way from the Strand to *Ath nan Corp*, the better part of two miles.

Hugh of the Glen's story, so whoever might be telling it would conclude, was simply one of a number of Colonsay examples of the 'second sight' – a vision of a future event – because many years later, during the early years of the First World War, the Royal Navy had conducted a major training exercise near Oronsay and a large party came ashore and marched together along precisely the same route that Hugh of the Glen and his companion had seen them take.

Another image comes to mind: of a much, much larger and totally unregimented crowd, gathered together on the machair in the summer sunshine, a bit like a giant version of a Colonsay Sports Day, groups of people blethering amiably to each other, the songs of the ascending skylarks all but lost behind the buzz of thousands of conversations coming from a fantastical reunion of the all-time, all-inclusive Colonsay community that reaches back to its human beginnings and stretches forward through countless generations to the present day and beyond. The story starts at least six thousand years ago with some of Colonsay's first first-footers, those Kiloran Bay cave dwellers, and then the Azilian settlers who, not long after the last ice sheet had retreated from the north of Europe, somehow ferried themselves across the intervening seas to find rich pickings along Oronsay's then higher-level shoreline and, over a period of many hundreds of years, created the huge shell middens which now feature as the grass-covered knolls, pockmarked with rabbit holes and their whelk and limpet shell-strewn entrances, that are dotted across the island.

The community includes too the hardly less mysterious Stone Age and Iron Age settlers who left their stone cist burials, standing stones and handful of discovered artefacts for us to ponder. And then came the hewers and builders of all those *Duns*, the rock-built fortresses, that stand sentinel across Colonsay as if just waiting for their chiefs and followers one day to return and restore them to their former positions of disputatious power and influence.

Then there were the seafaring holy men and women from Ireland who first came to Colonsay in their coracles at least fifteen hundred years ago, and brought with them a religion and a language and a culture whose defining influence has persisted right through the centuries to this day, notwithstanding a rude interruption or two from those entrepreneurial Norsemen who nevertheless ended up becoming absorbed into the predominant local culture – the ultimate destiny of all incomers.

It may only be a virtual community, but it has room for everyone who has ever set foot on the islands of Colonsay and Oronsay; marauding Vikings, Irish saints, Iron Age chieftains, prehistoric shell-gatherers, lairds, factors, transient potters, second-home owners, holidaymakers, festival-goers, locals of all ages past and present, including the great Colonsay diaspora comprising all those dispersed by time and circumstance who yet remain an intrinsic part of this great extended Colonsay family, tied for all time together by their common relationship with a very particular and special place, set in the southern Hebrides somewhere near the western horizon, stuffed full of ancestral memories, if only they were more accessible, and so many different stories and possibilities.

A bunch of the (1970s) boys to the rescue . . . or so the story goes.

> A bunch of the boys were quenching their thirst in Colonsay's lone Hotel,
> Wee Roger, Seaview, to name but a few, and Duncan and Davie as well.
> In his place near the door was our Para Mor who was sipping a pint of Light
> And telling the boys a story or two and generally keeping them right.
> When into the bar came another star, a giant of a man was he,
> With a loping stride about ten foot wide – or so it appeared to me.
> His name was Ross, called 'Hippo' too, he seemed hewn from ancient oak,
> Had hands like monstrous butterflies and his handshake was no joke.
> A nod to the Irishman manning the bar and Para had bought him a beer
> And with a *'Slainte mhaith, Pharuig'*★ Ross took a seat so the craic from the boys he could hear.
> But soon once again the door opened wide and in poured a sight for sore eyes,
> Wearing wellies of yellow, green, orange and blue and expressions of total surprise.
> The motley arrivals sat down by old Ross who'd just finished his pint with a wipe,
> And was carving some baccy from a block black as tar and carefully filling his pipe.
> 'Well, boys,' says he, 'you don't know me and none of you may give a damn,

But you look like the crew from the old Kangaroo and,
    ach well, I'll just take a dram.
And this here is Jum and, though you don't know hum,
    he's the best dog you'll find in this town –
Now, steady there, Jum, just be a flat dog,' and Jim lay
    obediently down
Though he kept a sharp eye on the basket of chips being
    scoffed by the men with the wellies
And when one fell to the floor he just stuck out a paw and
    joined them in filling their bellies.
The crew's leader was wearing a nautical cap that some-
    how just didn't belong –
They all looked so relieved to've discovered dry land you
    just *knew* something *had* to be wrong.
Their hired yacht, it turned out, had got stuck on a rock
    they'd discovered not far from the pier,
And they were hoping the problem might just go away if
    they went to the pub for a beer.
The boys at the bar thought the story bizarre and one that
    would lead to disaster,
So, not for the first time, they looked for their lead to the
    island's one only piermaster.
– Para Mor, it was he, slowly finished his pint and brush-
    ing some froth from his beard,
Said scarce a word but just gave them a look and out of
    the pub disappeared.
The boys followed fast and so did the rest for they'd
    guessed what was in Para's mind,
And Wee Roger too, Ross, Jim and old Hugh had no
    wish to be left behind.
So into the three-wheeler belonging to Hugh they
    squeezed like sardines in a can
And followed the cars on their way to the pier, led by
    Para's ex-post office van.
And soon one long rope they'd attached to the boat, the
    other end tied to the pier,

When up stepped old Ross and said '*Mach's a rathad,*[*] I
    think I'll just take it from here.'
And, living his legend, gave one mighty heave and she slid
    off the rock with a groan
And the crowd of onlookers could hardly believe that
    he'd managed it all on his own.
The man with the nautical cap proclaimed 'I say, old boy,
    that was super;
You've saved our boat and my bacon too – you are an
    ebbsolute trooper!'
He insisted they all return to the pub – an offer quite hard
    to decline –
And, as I recall, Ross spoke for us all when he said 'Ach
    well, mighty fine!'

. . .

'There are strange things done in the midnight sun,' as
    Ross was accustomed to mention,
And tales are still told of those great men of old and some
    are, of course, pure invention,
So welcome to Colonsay, land full of tales, where truth
    may be stranger than fiction,
To an island of memories, precious as gold, and stories
    beyond contradiction.

[*]*Slainte mhaith, Pharuig* is Gaelic for 'Good health, Peter' and
Mach's a rathad translates as '(Mind) out of the way'.

16

AIR SGATH AN EILEIN,
'FOR THE ISLAND'S SAKE'

Though I would be a happy man to be back again in the company of old friends, let alone the legion of new introductions, it is but a reverie and, in truth, the longer I lived in Colonsay the more interested I became in trying to do something practical about one or two of our real life community development problems rather than just opining fruitlessly from the sidelines. I left the island before achieving much more than discovering my new direction of travel, but hoping always to see my alma mater live well and prosper. So it seems only right that this self-reflecting tale should end by focusing in on its real and permanent central character, Colonsay, and the solid progress it has made on so many fronts – thanks, first and foremost, to the enormous amount of effort invested over the years by committed islanders, with much necessary and welcome help from external partners and not a lot from its long-departed potter and erstwhile aspiring activist who, thanks to everything Colonsay gave to him, was able to busy himself along similar lines, but elsewhere.

Only those old enough to remember what it was like to live in Colonsay's darker than necessary ages will fully appreciate the transformation to the island's electricity and water supplies – now both on the mains. Another massive infrastructure improvement is the upgrading of its publicly subsidised transport links. Getting to and from the island has never been easier, notwithstanding the best efforts of the weather, seemingly pepped up by global warming, to throw its occasional spanners in the works. Whereas only three sailings a week were timetabled back in the seventies, the ferry now calls every single day of the week in the summer and four days a week in winter, including some which nowadays go on to the mainland terminal of Kennacraig on the Mull of Kintyre, calling in at Port Askaig on the island of Islay to the south, before making the return trip. And although the new roll-on roll-off extension, another substantial piece of public investment in the island, was added to the pier at Scalasaig to let the now front and rear-loading ferries debouch and absorb their exchanges of vehicles, locals and holidaymakers still foregather together, though nowadays at the end of the harbour rather than at the head of the pier, to share in the eternal drama of the ferry boat's comings and goings.

An equal, if not more fundamental, change for the better has been the introduction of an air service from Connel Airport, near Oban. The direct flight takes a mere twenty-five minutes rather than the nearer two-and-a-half hour ferry journey and it is less subject to winter weather delays and cancellations than a stormbound ferry. The old grass landing-strip that undulated its deceptive way east to west across the golf course has been replaced by a properly levelled-out and metalled runway, and the regular Tuesday and Thursday flights are twice a day, making it possible for the first time to get to Oban for an appointment and catch a flight back home the same day. There are often extra flights on Saturdays and Sundays during term time to allow the Colonsay children at secondary school in Oban to get home for weekends as and when they request – a massive, civilising improvement to the old regime which made this aspect of family life so hard on children and parents alike.

A litmus test of the relative strength or fragility of any small rural community, not least one as remote as Colonsay, is the number of children attending the local primary school, and whether the school roll is rising or falling. The predominant demographic trend in deep rural Scotland is of an increasingly ageing population and fewer families with children. Colonsay is no exception, and though the primary school's numbers have remained fairly constant for many years at around half a dozen or so, the quality of education the children receive is superlative.

Young couples and the families they raise are at the very heart of what brings a sense of vitality and well-being to every small rural community, but they need two essentials – a good home and a way of making a reasonable living – in order to be able to make a decent life for themselves and settle properly into the place of their choosing. Affordable housing opportunities are an absolute prerequisite, and a major leap forward was made when the local Lorne and the Isles (now West Highland) Housing Association managed to secure the enhanced level of public subsidy required to allow them to build eight comfortable, though inevitably expensive to deliver, houses for locally affordable rents, over two phases, which have now blended into the *Chinn t-earr*, 'the east end', at the foot of the *Beannan*, 'the little Ben', next to the shop, post office and splendiferous village hall in Scalasaig. The only casualty was Old Peter's once high-hedged and prize-winning vegetable garden, his pride and joy flattened for the greater good – but he would surely have approved, albeit after an initial sniff. Unlike the five council houses secured in the seventies, but subsequently reduced to two by the Right to Buy, the Housing Association houses were always protected and, as such, are absolutely guaranteed to continue serving the community by housing successive generations of Colonsay residents both well and affordably. They are a long-term community asset, in other words, and surely worth every penny of the public and private investment required.

Whether a community needs any new housing (very few don't), what kind, how much and where depends on the local housing context, and Colonsay's has changed greatly over the last thirty years or so. A time-traveller couldn't miss the fundamental change to the housing stock, now doubled by over sixty new builds if you include a few conversions of former steadings. Not one new house was built during the 1970s or for many years before that, and even after one of the Estate's rented houses in

Kiloran was consumed in minutes by an awe-inspiring fire it was not replaced. A key reason for this striking new-build expansion was that the island's landlord, Colonsay Estate, following the lead of the Church of Scotland on its parcel of land around the manse, took the liberating decision to sell land and facilitate independent development: not just house plots to private individuals who not only aspired but could also afford to build homes for themselves but, every bit as significantly, bigger sites to publicly-funded bodies for social and economic development. Thus, the local Housing Association were able to build their eight houses and Highlands and Islands Enterprise to build five industrial units, which now provide bases for the island's electricity supplier, SSE, and new and successful local enterprises including a micro-brewery, a bookshop and publishing house and a popular cafe/restaurant.

But surely just as significant for the development of the Colonsay community and the subsequent flowering of its creative ambitions has been the Village Hall, built in Scalasaig at the Millennium to replace its timeworn Kiloran predecessor of fond and pleasurably hazy memories. While it is true that this spacious but intimate new hall, with its offset roof ridge and arching timbers suggesting an upturned Viking longship, would not and could not have been delivered without a massive injection of outside funding from the National Lottery and other sources, it would never even have got to daisy level had it not been for the huge determination, hard graft and considerable fundraising efforts of 'ordinary' Colonsay folk. Thus it is that the resident islanders, through their elected Hall Committee, now own and control the use of this key community asset and make full and varied community use of it, welcoming young, old and in-between wherever they may hail from.

The new hall provides the ideal setting for the island's trademark ceilidhs and concerts, which raise hundreds of pounds a go for a variety of charitable causes and, equally, give just as much authentic, old-fashioned pleasure to locals and visitors alike as they always did. But now, in its re-imagined incarnation, it hosts a whole new realm of cultural events in the form of four annual festivals: the April Book Festival which always receives rave reviews from visiting authors and attendees alike, the popular Festival of Spring which follows on from that, running for three weeks into the middle of May and comprising a wide variety of events including guided nature and history walks, arts and crafts as well as cooking and baking classes – and there is now an Autumn Festival fortnight in October which offers a similarly eclectic mix. The Rugby Festival in July is also increasingly popular and, like the Book Festival, owes its impetus and organisation to people who have second homes on the island.

The pathfinder, however, the pioneering festival, was the now renowned *Ceol Cholasa*, the September 'Colonsay Music' festival, which was launched back in 2008 as a means of enriching and sharing the island's culture and sense of togetherness by bringing the best professional musicians to the island to make great music, but also with the firm aim of enabling local and visiting musicians to go to workshops and make their own music on the same public platform as the pros, and then have some impromptu fun alongside each other in the informal sessions which carry on in the Hotel afterwards. It does justice to its motto of *'Leis an eilean, air sgath an eilein'*, 'With the island, for the sake of the island', and the 'feel-good festival' as Phil Cunningham christened it, is so popular now that it not only draws in visitors from far and wide, but provides an occasion for the reunion of people with Colonsay connections who live 'away', overtaking the once traditional homecoming at New Year, when it seemed like the Hogmanay ferry might capsize with the number of old friends and varied accomplices crowding cheerily to the side as their seasonal ship edged its way in alongside the welcoming pier.

To the festivals should be added the other events that are laid on by islanders with the express intention of celebrating what the island and its community have to offer, including traditional ones like the long-established Root and Grain Show, and new ones like the three-day Gathering in 2014, organised by the self-effacing but quietly thriving Colonsay and Oronsay Heritage Society, which celebrated and shared the life and accomplishments of Colonsay's very own Professor MacKinnon. The hard graft put in by the handful of people living in this tiny community in running these events is impressive enough, but it is the boldness of vision and the leap of imagination which has inspired them which marks the extent of the change in community self-belief and self-expression that, so it seems to me, has taken place since the late feudal, and much more diffident, period when my family lived in Colonsay. A starry-eyed old romantic might venture that this vision is as brilliantly outward-looking and inclusive as it is inwardly-driven by the need to give witness to just what life in this unique Hebridean community, with all its particular natural wonders and stories and attributes, means to those who live with and by them. A cynic might care to reflect that turning an ambitious dream into tangible reality is the hard bit, and by this acid test Colonsay's achievement in not just formulating but actually putting on so many very successful and different annual festivals, on top of everything else it does, provides solid testament to the resilience of its community spirit and the potential of its community ambition.

And that's not the half of it. The Gun Club, the Golf Club and the Sports Committee continue to offer entertainment to all-comers in their inimitable ways, and the ad hoc games of football, rugby and cricket ensure that the tranquillity of the machair will continue to be disturbed from time to time by loud bangs, cries of anguish, laughter and the occasional howzat; and though the Young Farmers Club eventually ran out of steam and members, the Root and Grain Show lives on, and badminton, music, drama and book clubs have sprung up like new shoots. The Colonsay Regatta, which like the Golf Course was no more than another 'tha cuin' agam', 'I remember . . .' talking point in the 1970s, was also resurrected with similar, 'let's just get on and do it' aplomb by Kevin Byrne. An *Oban Times* report on the 1866 regatta noted that 'The next race was for four-oared rowing boats and the course about a mile. After a gallant struggle a barge belonging to the Rt. Hon.

Duncan McNeill came in first and the "Hornet" belonging to Mr. McLeod of Kiloran a tolerable second. All the boats were well-greased and the broad belt of calm left in the wake of some showed that palm oil was cheap.' Nowadays the Regatta offers competitive fun for kayakers, raft-racers and swimmers as well as sailing enthusiasts, although no *Oban Times* reports have yet been filed as to how well-oiled present day Colonsay Regattas are by comparison.

More far-reaching in its potential still, the community decided in 2000 to set up its own Colonsay Community Development Company 'focused on the economic, social and environmental regeneration of the island'. It is a charitable company, with community-elected directors, and it has worked very hard to take on and overcome some of the most exciting, if daunting, of the island's community development challenges – and if it hasn't yet achieved everything it would like then, in my experience, that's the long-term nature of community development everywhere, and no small community should be anything other than applauded and encouraged when they respond to the challenge of endeavouring to shape their own destiny – even if they sometimes get less credit for their efforts than they surely deserve.

Its achievements to date, however, are considerable. It set up a subsidiary, the Colonsay Trading Company, to take over the island's fuel pumps and to ensure the island gets regular supplies of coal, bottled gas, petrol and diesel. In 2005 it took this asset-owning approach to community regeneration to another level when, with help from the Scottish Land Fund, the Development Company bought an area of Kilchattan croft land and created five new crofts on it to attract new residents to come and live on the island. Though not without some unanticipated crofting-law challenges, the project has resulted in the crofts being taken up by new crofters and brought welcome new households to settle on the island. Moreover, the Development Company are looking to get some additional affordable houses built on an unallocated portion of the remaining croft land they own.

Affordable housing was identified by a 2011 islander survey carried out by the Company's Development Officers as the single most important issue for the Development Company to address in order to deliver its strategic regeneration objective. So it decided to set its sights on acquiring and servicing another, much bigger, site in Scalasaig with enough room and forward development capacity to make possible the delivery of the mix of new, but locally affordable, homes that they believed the island would require in order, slowly but surely, to grow its small population – and along with it the island's job base and economy – over not just the short term but the medium to longer term. For this remains the most stubbornly resistant community development problem that Colonsay and Oronsay have had to live with since the early 1950s, when their combined population which, after a remorseless decline from its peak of nearly a thousand in the 1840s, seemed to settle at around the 250-mark or so during the first half of the twentieth century, but then fell away steadily yet again during the 1950s and 60s to its persistent all-time low of around half that, and sometimes even less during the decades which have followed. A community's greatest asset is the people who live in it, and a good-going, all-year-round community life rather than a more seasonally reliant one depends on there being enough socially and economically active people doing their individual and collective things in it to make it tick over happily.

Not that the two islands haven't been holding their own in unpropitious circumstances over recent years, with a combined 2011 Census increase to 132 permanently resident souls, but it still represents snail-like progress from the 128 when I made my first count in 1972, and it only takes a couple of households to decide to leave the island for the numbers to take a disheartening, if hopefully short-lived, dive again. It seems curious at first sight that this flatlining has persisted, given the remarkable level of new build that has taken place on the island, but there are countervailing factors at work. First, the demographic context: while Scotland's population has been steadily increasing, Argyll (and Bute)'s – Colonsay's local authority area – has been contracting faster than any other in Scotland and, in terms of age groups, the steep decline in the numbers of younger people in Argyll communities is matched only by the exponential growth in the numbers and proportion of older people; secondly, household sizes have been steadily shrinking everywhere, so whereas Colonsay needed about 50 houses to house its permanent population of two and a half times that number back in the seventies it now needs 60 to house just about the same number, because there are fewer households with children and more older-person, often single-person households.

In addition, while 25 of the newly built houses are lived in all the year round, the remainder are used by their owners and their families as second homes; but if they are not, then they are let out to holidaymakers. The big difference here is that whereas holiday homes were once the sole preserve of the islands' one and only landowner, Colonsay Estate, many other homeowners, whether they are permanently resident islanders or ex- or non-resident ones, have since been able to take similar economic advantage of Colonsay's biggest single economic driver – tourism – and many have done so, including a significant number of permanent residents who rely on this vital source of income.

The new-build boom delivered other significant community benefits, in that getting on for half of all the new houses were built by an island farmer and now expatriate book writer, Nigel Grant, and his team of various other locals. In addition, more than a dozen other houses and conversions have been self-builds, which means that, overall, most of the construction work on this increase in the housing stock was done by resident islanders. What's more, most of the workers and the mix of construction and allied trade skills they practised have stayed on the island and, no less importantly, the wages earned in the process went into the pockets of islanders, to the much more widespread benefit of the island economy.

Is there, nevertheless, any contradiction in the island now having created enough new housing to accommodate three times its number of permanent residents – when you add up all the visitors and their families who, at any one time, live on the island during their weeks-long summer season holidays – but somehow still not having available enough good and locally affordable homes on hand to enable the longer-term growth that the community has said that it needs and wants to see? The reality is that the island's economy and way of life are even more dependent on accommodating visitors today than when my own household's livelihood relied on holidaymakers buying my pots.

Employment patterns have been altering accordingly too. For example, where once all of the Estate's eight farms were lived in and worked by farming families, the farming workforce has steadily reduced, and all of the associated farmhouses have been vacated over time and turned into much more remunerative holiday lets. Though new crofts have been created and Colonsay's crofting tradition and practice live on still, albeit at similarly reducing levels of agricultural production, it too has been influenced by a big, subsidy-incentivised switch away from producing crops and livestock to delivering the different public policy objective of working the land even less intensively in order to improve the well-being of the island's fauna and flora. Colonsay and Oronsay environment-lovers, myself included, are happy to see special birds like the corncrake and the chough thrive as a consequence, but will have to wait and see whether such changes in land use will prove to have helped sustain, if not grow, the local population as effectively as they have the local vegetation and wildlife.

There has also been a big change in the way that Colonsay folk make a living from the seas that surround them. Lobster-creeling, which used to keep two or three small local boats busy from early summer to whenever the late autumn gales came and made discretion the better part of valour, is now little more than a recreation for one or two locals rather than the serious and skilled business it was for those dedicated fishermen who used to pursue it, and who, like the farming fraternity of yesteryear, were the repositories of a huge amount of priceless local knowledge, much of it passed down from generation to generation – and with a compendium of good stories to match, of course – about how and where Colonsay and Oronsay could get the best out of their two prime natural assets, the land and the sea. The lobsters haven't gone away, though, and nor have the independent income-earning opportunities they can still provide.

The oyster farm which Andrew Abrahams set up on the Strand in the seventies now exports oysters as well as home-grown honey all over the UK, but his instrumental contribution now extends to a landmark piece of legislation. The Bee-Keeping (Colonsay and Oronsay) Order 2013 has created a sanctuary for the native Black Bee which, though it knows how to survive and thrive in tough environmental conditions, needs safeguarding from the import and associated infectious dangers of other species of honey bee. Much more recently a multinational has established a fish-farm base on the island, and the salmon grown in the cages which now hug Colonsay's eastern shoreline presently provide some good, all-year-round local jobs which have brought new people to live on the island and, they suggest, could bring more.

An entrepreneur is someone who gets the spark of an idea, brews and stews it for a bit, takes a big decision to make a deeply personal project out of it and then commits a huge amount of thought, time, effort, angst and expense to getting it up and running, though usually not without a varying degree of assistance from other sympathetically-inclined people and bodies who support the ambition. By this definition today's Colonsay has plenty of local entrepreneurs – private, social and both – and plenty of good exemplars of home-grown entrepreneurial success, whether in the shape of new homes, festivals, bottled beers, black bees, publishing companies, community halls and development trusts, or in any of the other guises they happen to emerge; and surely they help to answer the often-asked community development question: which should come first, new jobs or new houses?

Entrepreneurs don't all have to be Bill Gates; they could just be an ordinary Joe or Joanna, some green and slightly hippified potter even, with an idea for making a living which they would like to try out in a place with a stunning environment and a good community and way of life for them and their family to thrive in. But first they will need a house they can call home. For the potter of a bygone era it was the availability of a humble cottage that provided the first, all-important stepping stone onto the island and into the welcoming embrace of the Colonsay community, moreover at a rental outlay even he could afford. Competing holiday accommodation pressures on any non-permanently occupied houses on the island mean that such stepping-stone houses would almost certainly have to be built with that sole purpose in mind. They could be located wherever a good, economically developable site is realistically available, but they could also form part of the mix of new housing opportunities which Colonsay's Community Development Company has previously said it would like to facilitate on the five-acre site in Scalasaig they were seeking to buy from Colonsay Estate. If the stone-steppers get happily established, then they could be offered adjacent house plots or other, more permanent, rented or shared equity housing opportunities there or elsewhere on the island; thus the stepping-stone houses would be freed up in due course to do the same thing again and thereby help grow the island population, bring new children into the Primary School, improve the island's overall demographic balance, expand its workforce and entrepreneurial possibilities, add to the craic and choice of partners at ceilidh dances, increase the cast-list of island characters and generally help keep the local community buzzing and its visitors interested and well looked after. *Air sgath an eilein.*

My tale is almost told, but before concluding it I wanted to see Colonsay and Oronsay once more in the very depth of winter, when the seasonal growth of vegetation and visitors has melted away and the bared basics of the place can be seen and felt more clearly. I flew in for my first time ever on a plane which happened to be piloted by an angel, Captain Julie Angell of Hebridean Airways, and the bird's-eye view she gave her passengers from the little eight-seater was close to miraculous. We passed very low, right over the top of the southernmost of the Isles of the Sea, *Eileach an Naoimh*, 'The Saint's Islet', and looked down on the beehive cells where St Columba and his monks used to take their sixth-century retreats under the watchful eye of his mother, Eithne, who is laid to rest there. Then, on down the length of the wild and totally deserted west coast of Jura to which, in perfect spring weather, Para Mor and I used occasionally to go over to for the day in his boat, after seeing off the 6 a.m. ferry, and gather up quantities of aluminium floats destined for a mainland scrap merchant, plus some seagull eggs to share out with the locals when we got home.

After landing on Islay we flew due north and low over Seal Island, Oronsay and Ardskenish, disturbing great flocks of over-wintering barnacle geese and filling my head with recollections of old friends and bygone ploys on land and sea. The angel treated the Machrins runway as if she naturally needed no more than a pin's head to alight upon, and me and the man from the Water Board stepped onto the tarmac like a couple of guys changing taxis; mine – Donald Garvard's music-making son, Peedie, still singing his way through life like a lintie – requiring its driver to finish his airport business first. We were soon joined in his office by the local crew of the fire tender and in an instant all was pure Colonsay again, as if I had never left, the islanders ever ready for a companionable blether, an eclectic exchange of info, some wry humour, the odd moan: it keeps you right at any time of the year and felt better than getting my passport stamped. It was good to be back.

REFERENCES

1. Professor Donald MacKinnon, 'Place Names and Personal Names in Argyll', 13 articles published in *The Scotsman* during November and December, 1887.

2. John de Vere Loder, *Colonsay and Oronsay in the Isles of Argyll* (Oliver & Boyd, 1935, reprinted in 1995 by Colonsay Press).

3. Murdoch McNeill, *Colonsay, One of the Hebrides*, (David Douglas, Edinburgh, 1910, reprinted in 2007 by Lightning Source Incorporated).

4. W.J. Watson, *The Celtic Placenames of Scotland* (William Blackwood, 1926, reprinted in 2011 by Birlinn Ltd).

5. I gratefully record my appreciation to the following resident and expatriate Colonsay and Oronsay people, native Colonsay-Gaelic speakers all, who helped me with my placename project when I lived in Colonsay during the 1970s: 'Donald Garvard' ('D.A.') McNeill, his brother 'Neilly', their sister, Flora McNeill and her husband Andrew ('A.S.') McNeill; Mary Clark and her nephews, John Clark and Angus Clark; brothers Neil and Ross Darroch; 'Aldy' MacAllister and his wife, Jessie (nee Brown); Finlay MacFadyen and his brother Angus; Maggie MacAllister, her brother, 'Old Peter' MacAllister, their nephew, 'Para Mor', 'Big Peter' MacAllister, Big Peter's brother, Johnnie MacAllister and their cousin, 'Duncan Sandy' MacAllister; 'Donald Gibby' McNeill and his brother 'Dotie' (Duncan) McNeill; Neil Martin and his sister, Mary Martin; 'Alastair Machrins' (Alastair McNeill); Jasper Brown and his wife, Katie Brown (née

MacAllister) and 'Morag Cholla' (Morag Titterton), who were both sisters of Aldy; Dolly Ann MacDougall and her daughter, Ina Williams; 'John a Gobha' (John MacIntyre); Hugh Galbraith; 'Ruaraidh Caol' ('Old Roger') MacIntyre and his son, 'Wee Roger' MacIntyre; Dougie MacGilvray; Duncan MacArthur, 'Duncan Balnahard' (Duncan McNeill); Archie McConnell and the many other Colonsay folk who used the local placenames in their conversation and responded gracefully to queries about them. Sadly, most of these good people have since died, though they live on happily in the memories of those that knew them

6. Other useful reference sources for the local placenames include all the Ordnance Survey Maps published of Colonsay and Oronsay, particularly the biggest scale and earliest (1880) 6-inch maps and also Kevin Byrne's *Placenames of Colonsay and Oronsay*, published by Colonsay Books, 1993, and his *Lonely Colonsay, Island at the Edge*, published by House of Lochar, 2010, which also contains a useful bibliography.